Emojis

and the Gospel of John

Copyright © 2018 by John Stahl

EMOJIs and the Gospel of John
Considering God's Feelings
by John Stahl

Email: EmojiGospel@gmail.com
Like us on Facebook: EMOJIs and the Gospel of John
Follow us on Twitter: @Pocket_Faith
Website: www.PocketFullOfFaith.com

Printed in the United States of America
Edited by Khrystal Khoury

ISBN 9780997425307 paperback
ISBN 9780997425314 eBook

Scripture is NOT copyrighted and is taken from the WEB (World English Bible). The WEB version of the Bible is meant for the public and neither the author or publishing company make any warrants to copyright this material. However, the author and publisher both appreciate and acknowledge the WEB for their efforts to share this version of the Bible freely. The Holy Bible is God's Word and it belongs to God.

Published in Ohio by Pocket Full of Faith Products in conjunction with Just Jesus Them Ministries.
www.PocketFullOfFaith.com

Cover Design by: CJ McDaniel
www.adazing.com

Interior Design by: George Dey
www.slimansprintery.com

In an effort to support local communities, raise awareness, and funds, Just Jesus Them Ministries donates a percentage of all book sales to local churches and ministries in (but not limited to) NorthEast Ohio.

EMOJIs used in license agreement with EMOJIONE.com. © 2018 EmojiOne

SPECIAL THANKS:

To Deanna and our kids, Chandler, Jacob, Nathan, and Rebecca. (A special shout out to Nate as this time he knew I was writing a book.)

To Vince and Lauri for making sure I ate the live frog every day. To Khrystal for editing. To Bobby and Danielle (aka Prickly Pete and Freak Dog) for the amazing videos. I already miss you guys. (You, too, Juniper Dee aka PerDee.) To Judi and George who believed in this project and were so kind in their effort and support! To John Morr for the web design and insight. To Rich and Karrie for their continued support in every project I attempt to accomplish for God.

To J-9 and (Master Ed) and the JSRV. Even though this isn't a true JSRV, the baseline was set years ago and hopefully it helps people go from here to their Bible, regardless of version. Thanks J-9!

To Keith, Rick, Ben and Lorie, Johnny and Kaitlyn, Ryan and Heather, Dallas, Brian Z, Howard Russell and his Christian Healthcare Ministries family, especially Joseph and Mark Russell, Josh, Tom, and those that have supported me along the path of ministry over the years. May you always be doers of the Word. Hearing only makes us complacent and lazy. Be the Word and do the Word!

To the folks at WEB (World English Bible) that understand the Bible is God's Word and He owns it. It is up to us to study and share it and live

it before others. I pray this book helps them do just that.

Learn It. Live It. Love others with It. What is "It"? The good news that God loves each of us so much that He sent His son Jesus so that we

may live this life to the fullest, both now and eternally.

Starting with the "Why?"

This book is not intended to replace the Bible. Nothing can do that. This is one piece of the Bible and is intended to help generations of all ages come together through the combination of God's Word and something that we all understand, use, and see almost every day: EMOJIs.

The intention is to take one piece of the Bible and help people understand it and share it with others. It is also meant to study this together and talk about the Word, the EMOJI tied to the Word, and, eventually, send us into the Bible to understand more of it.

We started with the Gospel of John because it is the universal gospel. It was meant for everyone. It shows and shares Jesus in a way the other gospels do not. It also has a couple of themes that we don't want you to miss: life and love. Focus on those themes as you read on, hopefully with someone by your side. You don't have to do it alone. In fact, you (ok, we) were never meant to!

Also, as you read, may you consider the feelings of others. May you consider the writer, the reader, the people in the book, and, most of all, God.

Lastly, the study notes may not be perfect. We did our best. But, God's Word is perfect, and the impact those words have on you (each of us) are, ultimately, what counts.

James 1:22.

The EMOJIS:		The emotion behind the EMOJIS:
	=	Wow! Astonished or shocked.
	=	Hmm... Think about it.
	=	Sadness.
	=	Alright! It's all good!
	=	Pay attention, God sent a messenger.
	=	Relieved.
	=	Grrrrr. Angry.
	=	Bible verse or numbers reference.
	=	This worries me.

Introduction to Chapter 1

The first chapter starts out by taking us back to the beginning of time, as we know it, which you can read in the Book of Genesis in the Old Testament. It continues with the general account of creation to the battle that we don't often consider: light versus dark. Did you know that there is no such thing as darkness? Darkness is just the absence of light. Whenever and wherever darkness is, once light enters, it pierces through and the darkness immediately vanishes. Darkness can't contain and can't defeat the light. It runs and hides completely. If you were to walk into a dark room with a flashlight or allow the light in from the room behind you, it would immediately take away any darkness that the light can touch.

Chapter one also introduces us to a person that many know of, history writes about, yet someone that has a very brief time in the Bible: John the Baptist or John the Baptizer. The only gospel that John the Baptist is NOT called John the Baptist is the Gospel of John. Why? We aren't sure, other than the author of this book, John, never refers to himself as "John", so, instead he refers to John the Baptist as "John".

The first chapter ends with Jesus calling his first disciples to walk alongside of Him. Remember, no one has heard from God directly in over 400 years. The newfound disciples are so overjoyed because they have found what everyone has been looking for and waiting on all that time: the Messiah.

The Good News According to John 😮

(From the Title page on the left) Which "John" wrote this gospel? The author is one of the 12 disciples of Jesus. You will see as we go through this book, he may have actually been Jesus's best friend on Earth.

John 1:1 The book of John was written to the Gentiles. If you are not a Jew than you are a Gentile. So how does the Book of John start to those of us that are Gentiles? The same way the Bible does in the Book of Genesis…"In the beginning…"

John 1:1-3 Notice that in the beginning the Word was **with** God and **was** God? This shows us that from the beginning God is a personal God. He was there for everything that was made, including you and me!

CHAPTER 1

In the beginning was the Word, and the Word was with God, and the Word was God. **2** The same was in the beginning with God. **3** All things were made through him. Without him, nothing was made that has been made. **4** In him was life, and the life was the light of men. **5** The light shines in the darkness, and the darkness hasn't overcome it. **6** There came a man, sent from God, whose name was John. **7** The same came as a witness; that he might testify about the light, that all might believe through him. **8** He was not the light, but was sent that he might testify about the light. **9** The true light that enlightens everyone was coming into the world.

10 He was in the world, and the world was made through him, and the world didn't recognize him. **11** He came to his own, and those who were his own didn't receive him.

👍 **12** But as many as received him, to them he gave the right to become God's children, to those who believe in his name; **13** who were born not of blood, nor of the will of the flesh, nor of the will of man, but of God. **14** The Word became flesh, and lived among us. We saw his glory, such glory as of the one and only Son of the Father, full of grace and truth. **15** John testified about him. He cried out, saying, "This was he of whom I said, 'He who comes after me has surpassed me, for he was before me.' " **16** From his fullness we all received grace upon grace.

👍 **17** For the law was given through Moses. Grace and truth were realized through Jesus Christ. **18** No one has seen God at any time. The one and only Son, who is in the bosom of the Father, has declared him.

😲 **19** This is John's testimony, when the Jews sent priests and Levites from Jerusalem to ask him, "Who are you?"

👍 John 1:12 What a small word: "But...". When you find it in the Bible, pause for a moment and see what happens next. In this case we get a promise from God (there are over 800 promises in the Bible!) – that each person who believes has the right to call himself or herself a child of God.

👍 John1:16 Here is an easy way to remember what God's grace means: G.R.A.C.E = God's Riches At Christ's Expense

😲 John 1:19 Notice who came first? It was John the Baptizer (also known as John the Baptist). He was the messenger. God first brought the message through John the Baptist. Then He sent the Messiah with Jesus.

John 1:19-21 In the Old Testament, God would speak to people through prophets. But, God hadn't spoken to anyone for over 400 years. The people were looking for someone to deliver them. That was the Messiah or the Christ. When John said that wasn't him, they thought he might be Elijah. Why? Elijah never actually died a physical death. So many people watched for his return.

John 1:25 When you see the word "Christ" it means the "Anointed One". "Jesus" means "God saves us". So, "Jesus Christ" literally means "the Anointed One that saves us".

20 He declared, and didn't deny, but he declared, "I am not the Christ."

21 They asked him, "What then? Are you Elijah?"

He said, "I am not."

"Are you the prophet?"

He answered, "No."

22 They said therefore to him, "Who are you? Give us an answer to take back to those who sent us. What do you say about yourself?"

23 He said, "I am the voice of one crying in the wilderness, 'Make straight the way of the Lord,' as Isaiah the prophet said."

24 The ones who had been sent were from the Pharisees. **25** They asked him, "Why then do you baptize, if you are not the Christ, nor Elijah, nor the prophet?"

26 John answered them, "I baptize in water, but among you stands one whom you don't know. **27** He is the one who comes after me, who is preferred before me, whose sandal strap I'm not worthy to loosen."

28 These things were done in Bethany beyond the Jordan, where John was baptizing. **29** The next day, he saw Jesus coming to him, and said, "Behold, the Lamb of God, who takes away the sin of the world! **30** This is he of whom I said, 'After me comes a man who is preferred before me, for he was before me.' 🔲 **31** I didn't know him, but for this reason I came baptizing in water: that he would be revealed to Israel."

32 John testified, saying, "I have seen the Spirit, descending like a dove out of heaven, and it remained on him. **33** I didn't recognize him, but he who sent me to baptize in water, he said to me, 'On whomever you will see the Spirit descending, and remaining on him, the same is he who baptizes in the Holy Spirit.' **34** I have seen, and have testified that this is the Son of God." 😮

35 Again, the next day, John was standing with two of his disciples, "Behold, the Lamb of God!"

🔲 John 1:30 This was the third time John the Baptist had told them that there was one coming after him who: 1. Has surpassed me (John 1:15); 2. "Whose sandals" John was not worthy to loosen (John 1:27); and 3. Was preferred before John and was before John. A common theme throughout the Gospels was when people talked, others really weren't listening, especially when it came to the voice of God.

😮 John 1:34 When John called Jesus the "Lamb of God" he was talking to a Jewish crowd. They understood that a lamb was used as a sacrifice, as this was done daily in the temple. When John also revealed that Jesus was the "Son of God" he was letting this same Jewish crowd know that the sacrifice God was about to make was his very own Son.

John 1:38 The first time we hear Jesus speak in the Book of John is with a question. Jesus was the master at asking questions. They were always pointed and meaningful. His first question to these disciples is the first question you and I could answer when it comes to our relationship with Jesus: What are you looking for? It's a personal question that comes with a unique answer.

John 1:38 This is typical of the disciples. It is also typical of you and me today. Jesus asks a simple question and they answer a question that was never asked! Notice, too, Jesus didn't ask "WHO" they were looking for, Jesus asked "WHAT".

John 1:39 The Jewish day started at 6 a.m. so the tenth hour would be ten hours later, or 4 p.m.

36 and he looked at Jesus as he walked, and said, **37** The two disciples heard him speak, and they followed Jesus. **38** Jesus turned and saw them following, and said to them, "What are you looking for?"

They said to him, "Rabbi" (which is to say, being interpreted, Teacher), "where are you staying?"

39 He said to them, "Come, and see."
They came and saw where he was staying, and they stayed with him that day. It was about the tenth hour. **40** One of the two who heard John and followed him was Andrew, Simon Peter's brother. **41** He first found his own brother, Simon, and said to him, "We have found the Messiah!" (which is, being interpreted, Christ). **42** He brought him to Jesus. Jesus looked at him, and said, "You are Simon the son of Jonah. You shall be called Cephas" (which is by interpretation, Peter).

⁴³ On the next day, he was determined to go out into Galilee, and he found Philip. Jesus said to him, "Follow me." ⁴⁴ Now Philip was from Bethsaida, of the city of Andrew and Peter. ⁴⁵ Philip found Nathanael, and said to him, "We have found him, of whom Moses in the law, and the prophets, wrote: Jesus of Nazareth, the son of Joseph." ⁴⁶ Nathanael said to him, "Can any good thing come out of Nazareth?"

Philip said to him, "Come and see."

⁴⁷ Jesus saw Nathanael coming to him, and said about him, "Behold, an Israelite indeed, in whom is no deceit!"

⁴⁸ Nathanael said to him, "How do you know me?"

Jesus answered him, "Before Philip called you, when you were under the fig tree, I saw you."

⁴⁹ Nathanael answered him, "Rabbi, you are the Son of God! You are King of Israel!"

John 1:43 Jesus's instruction to Philip was very simple: "Follow me". It was up to Philip to choose to listen or go on his way. It's the same instruction God gives to each of us. You and I, like Philip, have to choose whether or not to follow. Choose wisely!

John 1:46 Nathanael showed that he had knowledge of the Scriptures. He knew that the Messiah would come from Bethlehem. And he knew the specific Bethlehem according to the book of Micah. This also meant that he would know that those same Scriptures taught us that God is good. How could the Messiah come from this little town in Nazareth? He knew the Scriptures, but he didn't know the full story behind Jesus and his birth.

John 1:51 Notice what the angels are doing? They are going up and down and back and forth from Heaven to Earth. Angels don't just live and stay in heaven. They also come back to Earth and minister to us.

50 Jesus answered him, "Because I told you, 'I saw you underneath the fig tree,' do you believe? You will see greater things than these!" **51** He said to him, "Most certainly, I tell you all, hereafter you will see heaven opened, and the angels of God ascending and descending on the Son of Man."

Introduction to Chapter 2

We see a shift in chapter two. Jesus has just gone public with His ministry. His disciples are alongside of Him. He attends a large wedding held by a well-known family that is wealthy. It is here that we see Jesus perform His first
 public, and possibly most controversial, miracle.

Why the controversy? Jesus turned water into wine. 😮 It leads to so many questions still to this day.

Is it ok to drink wine?

Is the wine alcoholic or non-alcoholic?

Is Jesus causing others to stumble because He is attending this ceremony, as it is nothing more than a big party? 🤔

None of these stop Jesus in his public ministry. None of these should stop us, either, as this subject takes us away from what is really important and why Jesus came to be with us: love and life. 😌

John 2:1-11 This is the story of the first public miracle at the beginning of Jesus's ministry. Look at what took place: it didn't happen in a temple or place of worship. It took place at a feast. It wasn't in front of all the religious people. It was in front of the common man. The conversion was done inside the pots of water. The celebration was a joyous one and the change from water into wine was one that wouldn't be changed back. Such is the life of the true believer. The change takes place on the inside. When others experience the change, people can't help but wonder how it happened.

John 2:4 Jesus said "My hour has not yet come" nine times in the first 17 chapters in the Gospel of John. If you are struggling in your walk, know this: when you trust God completely, your hour, too, will come!

CHAPTER 2

The third day, there was a wedding in Cana of Galilee. Jesus' mother was there. **2** Jesus also was invited, with his disciples, to the wedding. **3** When the wine ran out, Jesus' mother said to him, "They have no wine."

4 Jesus said to her, "Woman, what does that have to do with you and me? My hour has not yet come."

5 His mother said to the servants, "Whatever he says to you, do it." **6** Now there were six water pots of stone set there after the Jews' way of purifying, containing two or three metretes apiece. **7** Jesus said to them, "Fill the water pots with water." So they filled them up to the brim. **8** He said to them, "Now draw some out, and take it to the ruler of the feast." So they took it. **9** When the ruler of the feast tasted the water now become wine, and didn't know where it came from (but the servants who had drawn the water knew), the ruler of the feast called the bridegroom

10 and said to him, "Everyone serves the good wine first, and when the guests have drunk freely, then that which is worse. You have kept the good wine until now!" **11** This beginning of his signs Jesus did in Cana of Galilee, and revealed his glory; and his disciples believed in him.

12 After this, he went down to Capernaum, he, and his mother, his brothers 😮, and his disciples; and they stayed there a few days. **13** The Passover of the Jews was at hand, and Jesus went up to Jerusalem. **14** He found in the temple those who sold oxen, sheep, and doves, and the changers of money sitting. **15** He made a whip of cords, and threw all out of the temple, both the sheep and the oxen; and he poured out the changers' money and overthrew their tables. **16** To those who sold the doves, he said, "Take these things out of here! Don't make my Father's house a marketplace!" 😮 **17** His disciples remembered that it was written, "Zeal for your house will eat me up."

😮 John 2:12 Many people think Mary had Jesus and he was her only child. This verse shows us that Jesus was part of a family with siblings, like many of us are! The book of James and Jude in the New Testament are two of the siblings of Jesus!

😮 John 2:14-16 The outside area of the temple was a place for the common person. Male and female, adults and children, Jew and Gentile (a Gentile was any race or nationality that was not Jewish) were welcome in this area to pray and learn more about God. The priests turned this outer area into a marketplace. They had taken a place of prayer and worship and turned it into a place to make money. That is why Jesus turned over their tables. It isn't money that is the root of all evils. It is the *LOVE* of money. Jesus said you can only serve one master, and he knew the two choices to serve were God and money (Mt 6:24/Luke 16:13).

👍 John 2:23 There were only two places that Jesus was present in John Chapter 2: the house of the common man and the house of God. He was also present at two important Jewish ceremonies: a wedding (at the house, which was common in this culture) and Passover (at God's house. See note on John 13:1).

😶 John 2:23-25 It was easy for others to believe in Jesus when he was performing miracles and healing people. When times got difficult and the signs didn't happen as often, people pulled away from Jesus. Sadly, that is human nature, and Jesus knew this.

18 The Jews therefore answered him, "What sign do you show us, seeing that you do these things?"

19 Jesus answered them, "Destroy this temple, and in three days I will raise it up."

20 The Jews therefore said, "It took forty-six years to build this temple! Will you raise it up in three days?" **21** But he spoke of the temple of his body. **22** When therefore he was raised from the dead, his disciples remembered that he said this, and they believed the Scripture, and the word which Jesus had said. **23** Now when he was in Jerusalem at the Passover 👍, during the feast, many believed in his name, observing his signs which he did. **24** But Jesus didn't entrust himself to them, because he knew everyone, **25** and because he didn't need for anyone to testify concerning man; for he himself knew what was in man. 😶

Introduction to Chapter 3

This is the most pivotal chapter of the New Testament. We are introduced to a man named Nicodemus, who we will find to be a rich, religious leader. On a rooftop in the middle of the busiest time of the year in Jerusalem, a rabbi and The Rabbi meet. 😮 The two speak as The Feast of Passover is taking place. Jews from every country make the journey to their holy city still to this day. It is one of the seven feasts 🎴 that is celebrated every year in Jerusalem, and of those seven, is the most attended.

In verse 16, we hear the most famous verse to any believer, and one that we often share. 😌 It is God's mission statement to us all 😕, in just 26 words. 🎴 In verse 17 we see the follow up to verse 16, and one we often forget to share. 🙄 This verse is God's vision for us all, in just 22 words. 🎴

These two verses go hand in hand. They need each other, just as much as any non-believer needs to learn the importance of both verses.

Finally, this chapter ends as two of the most studied, controversial, and intriguing people in history, John the Baptist and Jesus, meet face to face. Where and why does this happen? Read on to find the answer! 👍

John 3:1-2 Here are some things to know about Nicodemus: he was rich (see notes on John 19:39), he was religious (he was a Pharisee), and he was a ruler. Being a ruler meant he was part of the Sanhedrin, which was the highest court of the Jews.

John 3:8 No one has seen the wind. We have only seen the effects of the wind. Whether it be branches and leaves in the trees, snow across a road or field, or the aftermath of a storm, we can't see the beginning or end of the wind. We can only see what the wind did to change an object. The same can be said for God's Spirit. We can't see His Spirit. But, we can see the effect it has on someone who believes. We can't tell when or where the Spirit began to make the change. But we can definitely see the changes made to all those who believe.

CHAPTER 3

Now there was a man of the Pharisees named Nicodemus, a ruler of the Jews. **2** The same came to him by night , and said to him, "Rabbi, we know that you are a teacher come from God, for no one can do these signs that you do, unless God is with him."

3 Jesus answered him, "Most certainly, I tell you, unless one is born anew, he can't see God's Kingdom."

4 Nicodemus said to him, "How can a man be born when he is old? Can he enter a second time into his mother's womb, and be born?"

5 Jesus answered, "Most certainly I tell you, unless one is born of water and spirit, he can't enter into God's Kingdom. **6** That which is born of the flesh is flesh. That which is born of the Spirit is spirit. **7** Don't marvel that I said to you, 'You must be born anew.' **8** The wind blows where it wants to, and you hear its sound, but don't know where it comes from and where it is going. So is everyone who is born of the Spirit." **9** Nicodemus answered him, "How can these things be?" **10** Jesus answered him, "Are you the teacher of Israel, and don't understand these things? **11** Most certainly I tell you, we speak that which we know, and testify of that which we have seen, and you don't receive our witness. **12** If I told you earthly things and you don't believe, how will you believe if I tell you heavenly things? **13** No one has ascended into heaven but he who descended out of heaven, the Son of Man, who is in heaven. **14** As Moses lifted up the serpent in the wilderness, even so must the Son of Man be lifted up, **15** that whoever believes in him should not perish, but have eternal life. **16** For God so loved the world, that he gave his one and only Son, that whoever believes in him should not perish, but have eternal life.

John 3:16 The most famous and pointed verse in the Bible. Yet, sadly, not the most quoted verse. That belongs to Matthew 7:1 "Don't judge so that you won't be judged."

John 3:16 In 25-26 words (depending on the Bible), God sums up his reason for coming to this world. We get to see His heart, His plan, and His will in our life in these words. What would your life look like in 25-26 words that would match God's heart, plan, and will?

John 3:16 Doesn't it make sense that the most famous verse in the Bible would come from Jesus's mouth and be heard by a massive crowd in an arena or stadium? Instead, it was to Nicodemus, a religious, non-believer, who was searching. He knew there was something missing, and he found it in this Rabbi he was talking to on a rooftop, where he found the Messiah, the savior of the world.

John 3:17 Jesus follows the most famous verse with a verse that should be more famous. He answers the question: "Why?" God didn't send his son to beat us up, put us down, judge, or condemn us. He sent his son to save us from our self and this world and live with him forever.

John 3:19 It has been said that the same sunlight that melts ice also hardens clay. Those that have a tender heart will respond to God's message of love. Those that harden their heart will continue to do what they choose, apart from God. This comes with a biblical warning: Pharaoh chose to harden his heart against God. Eventually, God hardened his heart completely (Exodus 10:27).

17 For God didn't send his Son into the world to judge the world, but that the world should be saved through him. **18** He who believes in him is not judged. He who doesn't believe has been judged already, because he has not believed in the name of the one and only Son of God. **19** This is the judgment, that the light has come into the world, and men loved the darkness rather than the light; for their works were evil. **20** For everyone who does evil hates the light, and doesn't come to the light, lest his works would be exposed. **21** But he who does the truth comes to the light, that his works may be revealed, that they have been done in God."

22 After these things, Jesus came with his disciples into the land of Judea. He stayed there with them and baptized. **23** John also was baptizing in Enon near Salim, because there was much water there. They came, and were baptized; **24** for John was not yet thrown into prison.

25 Therefore a dispute arose on the part of John's
disciples with some Jews about purification. **26** They came to John and said to him, "Rabbi, he who was with you beyond the Jordan, to whom you have testified, behold, he baptizes, and everyone is coming to him."

27 John answered, "A man can receive nothing unless it has been given him from heaven. **28** You yourselves testify that I said, 'I am not the Christ,' but, 'I have been sent before him.' **29** He who has the bride is the bridegroom; but the friend of the bridegroom, who stands and hears
him, rejoices greatly because of the bridegroom's voice. This, my joy, therefore is made full. **30** He must increase, but I must decrease. **31** He who comes from above is above all. He who is from the earth belongs to the earth and speaks of the earth. He who comes from heaven is above all. **32** What he has seen and heard, of that he testifies; and no one receives his witness. **33** He who has received his witness has

John 3:22-30 The disputes were beginning by the religious people over the rules. The man we know as John the Baptist will soon be thrown into prison. He was their rabbi and teacher at this time. But John stopped them in their tracks and pointed them to the one that is greater than he. He also shared a verse (John 3:30) that we should all remember and challenge ourselves to live daily: "He must increase, I must decrease." John was saying, "More of God. Less of me." It wasn't an option. It's a principle he had lived his entire life to date, and would continue to live until he was thrown into prison and had his life taken from him (Matthew 14:1-12).

😌 John 3:34 In Jeremiah 29:14 it says that when we seek God wholeheartedly – with our WHOLE hart – we will find Him. Here we see that when God gives his Spirit he gives it without measure. In John 3:16 we learned that God gave "His one and only Son...". When God gives to each one of us, He is all in, 100%, at all times, everywhere.

set his seal to this, that God is true. **34** For he whom God has sent speaks the words of God; for God gives the Spirit without measure. 😌 **35** The Father loves the Son, and has given all things into his hand. **36** One who believes in the Son has eternal life, but one who disobeys the Son won't see life, but the wrath of God remains on him."

Introduction to Chapter 4

The disciples have just started into full time ministry with a Rabbi that no one even knew just a short time before the Passover Feast. So, where does this Rabbi decide to go? Jesus purposefully decides to walk through Samaria and stops in the middle of the day at the well in the center of the city.

The Jews did not like the Samaritans.

The disciples head off to buy food, as they are hungry. In this chapter we get to see the human side of Jesus and He, like His disciples, is hot, tired, hungry, and thirsty as it is the middle of the day. When the disciples come back, they find him at the well not only talking to a Samaritan, but a Samaritan woman.

That is unheard of in this culture.

But, as we will soon see, that is also part of who Jesus is.

The well that Jesus rests at isn't just any well, either. This is Jacob's well (from where Jacob lived according to Genesis 33:19). The woman at the well asks Jesus if he is greater than Jacob? Jesus responds by sharing, for the first time, not to the crowds, the religious people, or even His disciples, that He is the one that generation after generation have been seeking.

Jesus is the Christ, the Messiah.

John 4:1 Whenever you see the word "therefore" in the Bible you should stop and ask yourself: "What in the world is that there for...? In this case, we start to see the very reason the Pharisees dislike and eventually hate Jesus. It wasn't about the words Jesus shared; it was about competition in the number of baptisms of disciples, which could threaten their very existence as a religious power.

John 4:6 This is the sixth hour, which means it is noon (See note on John 1:39), when the sun reaches its highest point and one of the hottest parts of any day.

John 4:6-8 Here we get to see the human side of Jesus that we often overlook. He sat down because he was tired from the journey. He wanted a drink because he was thirsty. The disciples went to get food for them because all of them were hungry.

CHAPTER 4

Therefore when the Lord knew that the Pharisees had heard that Jesus was making and baptizing more disciples than John **2** (although Jesus himself didn't baptize, but his disciples), **3** he left Judea and departed into Galilee. **4** He needed to pass through Samaria. **5** So he came to a city of Samaria, called Sychar, near the parcel of ground that Jacob gave to his son, Joseph. **6** Jacob's well was there. Jesus therefore, being tired from his journey, sat down by the well. It was about the sixth hour. **7** A woman of Samaria came to draw water. Jesus said to her, "Give me a drink." **8** For his disciples had gone away into the city to buy food.

9 The Samaritan woman therefore said to him, "How is it that you, being a Jew, ask for a drink from me, a Samaritan woman?" (For Jews have no dealings with Samaritans.)

10 Jesus answered her, "If you knew the gift of God, and who it is who says to you, 'Give me a drink,' you would have asked him, and he would have given you living water." 😮

11 The woman said to him, "Sir, you have nothing to draw with, and the well is deep. So where do you get that living water? **12** Are you greater than our father, Jacob, who gave us the well and drank from it himself, as did his children and his livestock?"
13 Jesus answered her, "Everyone who drinks of this water will thirst again, **14** but whoever drinks of the water that I will give him will never thirst again; but the water that I will give him will become in him a well of water springing up to eternal life." 😌 **15** The woman said to him, "Sir, give me this water, so that I don't get thirsty, neither come all the way here to draw."
16 Jesus said to her, "Go, call your husband, and come here."

😮 John 4:7-29 In chapter three, Jesus had a conversation at night with Nicodemus, a religious man who was calm, cool and collected. Nicodemus approached Jesus and spoke first. In chapter four, Jesus met a nameless woman in the heat of the day who was both fiery and ready to debate. Here, Jesus started the discussion. God will meet us at any time, anywhere, and is willing to listen and speak to each and every one of us. That is the loving savior we serve and who loves and serves us!

😌 John 4:15-26 Notice that Jesus is having a conversation with the woman? He isn't yelling at her or talking down to her. He is talking to her as you and I would talk to each other. The conversation is not just about the here and now. Jesus talks to her about eternity. It's the most important conversation of the woman at the well's life.

John 4:19 Imagine the surprise this woman must have had when Jesus knew the biggest problem she faced in her life. What did she do when she heard Jesus's words? She changed the subject. Many times we don't want to talk about where we miss the mark with God (which is the definition of "sin"), so when it hits us personally, the easiest thing to do is talk about something else!

John 4:24 God is spirit. We don't often think about that. This is how God is able to be everywhere, all the time. It is also why we can worship him anywhere at anytime.

17 The woman answered, "I have no husband."

Jesus said to her, "You said well, 'I have no husband,' **18** for you have had five husbands; and he whom you now have is not your husband. This you have said truly."

19 The woman said to him, "Sir, I perceive that you are a prophet. **20** Our fathers worshiped in this mountain, and you Jews say that in Jerusalem is the place where people ought to worship."

21 Jesus said to her, "Woman, believe me, the hour comes, when neither in this mountain, nor in Jerusalem, will you worship the Father. **22** You worship that which you don't know. We worship that which we know; for salvation is from the Jews. **23** But the hour comes, and now is, when the true worshipers will worship the Father in spirit and truth, for the Father seeks such to be his worshipers. **24** God is spirit, and those who worship him must worship in spirit and truth."

25 The woman said to him, "I know that Messiah ⊞ comes, he who is called Christ. When he has come, he will declare to us all things."

26 Jesus said to her, "I am he, the one who speaks to you." **27** At this, his disciples came. They marveled that he was speaking with a woman; yet no one said, "What are you looking for?" or, "Why do you speak with her?" 😮

28 So the woman left her water pot, went away into the city, and said to the people, **29** "Come, see a man who told me everything that I did. Can this be the Christ?"

30 They went out of the city, and were coming to him. **31** In the meanwhile, the disciples urged him, saying, "Rabbi, eat."

32 But he said to them, "I have food to eat that you don't know about."

⊞ John 4:25 All of Israel had been searching for the Messiah. They hadn't heard from God in over 400 years. The disciples of John the Baptist were the first to recognize Jesus as the Messiah (John 1:41). The second to recognize Jesus as the Messiah in the Gospel of John is a woman who was so ashamed, to the point she had to get water at a time of day, noon, when she knew no one else would be at the well.

😮 John 4:27 Remember that when the disciples showed back up to bring food to Jesus, that one of those disciples would have been John, the author of this gospel. In this culture, speaking to a woman, especially a Samaritan woman (see verse nine), was something that was simply not done. This is God showing He will cross any cultural boundary to show how much He loves everyone, regardless of race, nationality, or gender.

John 4:31-33 This is a perfect picture of the disciples. So many times in the Gospels you will see them focus on the here and now when Jesus is trying to help them focus eternally. He wasn't feeding them to fill them for an hour or a day. He wanted to fill them with the bread of life for eternity.

John 4:39-41 This is a very brief statement but a very important one. There were three regions to Israel at this time: Judea in the north, Galilee in the south, and Samaria in the middle. When Assyria had invaded Israel over 700 years before this, they took some of the Jewish women as their own. The children from these marriages were the Samaritans. Knowing that someone from Samaria had found the Messiah before them was too much for a "true" Jew to allow in their hearts and mind. It would further increase their hatred toward the Samaritans. It also created further animosity toward Jesus.

33 The disciples therefore said to one another, "Has anyone brought him something to eat?"

34 Jesus said to them, "My food is to do the will of him who sent me and to accomplish his work. **35** Don't you say, 'There are yet four months until the harvest?' Behold, I tell you, lift up your eyes and look at the fields, that they are white for harvest already. **36** He who reaps receives wages and gathers fruit to eternal life; that both he who sows and he who reaps may rejoice together. **37** For in this the saying is true, 'One sows, and another reaps.' **38** I sent you to reap that for which you haven't labored. Others have labored, and you have entered into their labor."

39 From that city many of the Samaritans believed in him because of the word of the woman, who testified, "He told me everything that I did." **40** So when the Samaritans came to him, they begged him to stay with them.

He stayed there two days. **41** Many more believed because of his word. **42** They said to the woman, "Now we believe, not because of your speaking; for we have heard for ourselves, and know that this is indeed the Christ, the Savior of the world." **43** After the two days he went out from there and went into Galilee. **44** For Jesus himself testified that a prophet has no honor in his own country. **45** So when he came into Galilee, the Galileans received him, having seen all the things that he did in Jerusalem at the feast, for they also went to the feast. **46** Jesus came therefore again to Cana of Galilee, where he made the water into wine. There was a certain nobleman whose son was sick at Capernaum. **47** When he heard that Jesus had come out of Judea into Galilee, he went to him, and begged him that he would come down and heal his son, for he was at the point of death.

John 4:46, 48 The word "therefore". Remember to stop at this word and ask yourself "What is that there for...? Something big is about to happen! (See note on john 4:1)

John 4:45-54 Just as there were seven "I AM..." statements that Jesus defined (See note on John 6:35), there are also seven miracles in the Gospel of John (John 2:11; John 4:46-54; John 5:1-15; John 6:5-14; John 6:16-24; John 9:1-7; John 11:1-45). This passage notes the second miracle of Jesus's public ministry (See note on John 2:1-11 for the first miracle.) Seven is the number of completion, as in seven days to create the world, seven days in our week, seven things the Lord detests (Proverbs 6:16), and others. In this case, the healing came in the seventh hour (around 1 p.m., see note on John 1:39).

John 4:54 In the book of John, miracles were "signs". The son of this nobleman was both sick and appeared to be terminal (verse 49). The people needed to "see" the sign. Jesus healed the boy without "seeing" him face to face. It took a day for this nobleman to realize this, at which point Jesus had already left the region. Many times faith isn't seeing, but, as in this case, believing.

⁴⁸ Jesus therefore said to him, "Unless you see signs and wonders, you will in no way believe."

⁴⁹ The nobleman said to him, "Sir, come down before my child dies." ⁵⁰ Jesus said to him, "Go your way. Your son lives." The man believed the word that Jesus spoke to him, and he went his way. ⁵¹ As he was now going down, his servants met him and reported, saying "Your child lives!" ⁵² So he inquired of them the hour when he began to get better. They said therefore to him, "Yesterday at the seventh hour, the fever left him." ⁵³ So the father knew that it was at that hour in which Jesus said to him, "Your son lives." He believed, as did his whole house. ⁵⁴ This is again the second sign that Jesus did, having come out of Judea into Galilee.

Introduction to Chapter 5

Jesus is heading to Jerusalem and stops off at a pool that the sick are sitting by, hoping to get well. An angel would stir the water and the first one in the water would be healed. A man who has been paralyzed for 38 years can't get himself in the pool, but Jesus heals Him, and tells him to get up, grab his bed and walk. Because of this, the Jews want to kill Jesus. In a poolside full of sick, paralyzed, blind, and lame people, Jesus heals one of them, and the Jews want to kill Him.

Why?

Because of the day Jesus did this miracle. It was the Sabbath and no one should work on that day. It was the rule.

Such is the hypocrisy of the Jews of this time. Many of the sick people had to be walked to or placed by the pool that day, which would be considered work. Someone had to lay the bed down for the paralyzed man to be placed on, which would also be work. The angel would stir the water at a certain time, which, by rule, would also be work.

When they came to Jesus about this, He was very direct. My Father (God) is at work, which means I am at work. In other words, Jesus had a world to save, and if God was doing what only God could do, than Jesus was taking His part in this, too, as they are one.

Talk like this would eventually cost Jesus his life, and Jesus knew it.

John 5:2-3
"Bethesda" means
house of mercy. The
people there had no
power over their
infirmity. The only way
to heal them was
through God's power. A
great multitude showed
up every day hoping for
God's mercy and his
power of healing to
touch them personally.

John 5:4 Further
proof that angels are
amongst us every day!
(See note on John 1:51)
Hebrews 1:14 tells us
angels are sent to serve
and minister to those of
us who are believers!

After these things, there was a feast of the Jews, and Jesus went up to Jerusalem. **2** Now in Jerusalem by the sheep gate, there is a pool, which is called in Hebrew, "Bethesda", having five porches. **3** In these lay a great multitude of those who were sick, blind, lame, or paralyzed, waiting for the moving of the water; **4** for an angel went down at certain times into the pool and stirred up the water. Whoever stepped in first after the stirring of the water was healed of whatever disease he had. **5** A certain man was there who had been sick for thirty-eight years. **6** When Jesus saw him lying there, and knew that he had been sick for a long time, he asked him, "Do you want to be made well?"

7 The sick man answered him, "Sir, I have no one to put me into the pool when the water is stirred up, but while I'm coming, another steps down before me."

8 Jesus said to him, "Arise, take up your mat, and walk."

9 Immediately, the man was made well, and took up his mat and walked.

Now it was the Sabbath on that day. **10** So the Jews said to him who was cured, "It is the Sabbath. It is not lawful for you to carry the mat."

11 He answered them, "He who made me well said to me, 'Take up your mat and walk.'"

12 Then they asked him, "Who is the man who said to you, 'Take up your mat and walk'?"

13 But he who was healed didn't know who it was, for Jesus had withdrawn, a crowd being in the place. **14** Afterward Jesus found him in the temple, and said to him, "Behold, you are made well. Sin no more, so that nothing worse happens to you."

15 The man went away, and told the Jews that it was Jesus who had made him well.

John 5:5-15 This is the third of seven miracles in the Gospel of John. (See note for all seven miracles, or signs, in John 4:45-54)

John 5:5-13 Isn't this human nature? A man that has been sick for 38 years runs into a religious person that was making sure no one was "working" on the Sabbath. The man was made well by Jesus and did as Jesus said. When the Jews saw that the man was made well and carried his mat, they stopped him to enforce their rule. Sadly, their focus wasn't on the man that was healed, rather, the mat that he carried that day.

John 5:16 To further share the extreme hatred the Jews were developing toward Jesus, we need to go no further than verse 16. Because Jesus healed a man on the Sabbath, a man that had been dealing with some kind of infirmity for 38 years, they wanted to kill him. They didn't want Jesus to pay a fine, write a note of apology, or even have him thrown in prison. They wanted him dead.

John 5:18 Eventually, this will be the reason the Jews will use to have Jesus hung on the cross to die. Jesus will heal the sick, make the blind see, and even raise people from the dead. But to call himself the Son of God is against everything the Jews teach and believe. He is claiming deity. The penalty for this is death. Remember, too, that Jesus knows this, and has the courage to speak it anyway. Jesus is well aware that this is part of God's will for His time here on Earth.

16 For this cause the Jews persecuted Jesus, and sought to kill him, because he did these things on the Sabbath. **17** But Jesus answered them, "My Father is still working, so I am working, too." **18** For this cause therefore the Jews sought all the more to kill him, because he not only broke the Sabbath, but also called God his own Father, making himself equal with God.

19 Jesus therefore answered them, "Most certainly, I tell you, the Son can do nothing of himself, but what he sees the Father doing. For whatever things he does, these the Son also does likewise. **20** For the Father has affection for the Son, and shows him all things that he himself does. He will show him greater works than these, that you may marvel. **21** For as the Father raises the dead and gives them life, even so the Son also gives life to whom he desires. **22** For the Father judges no one, but he has given all judgment to the Son,

23 that all may honor the Son, even as they honor the Father. He who doesn't honor the Son doesn't honor the Father who sent him.

24 "Most certainly I tell you, he who hears my word and believes him who sent me has eternal life, and doesn't come into judgment, but has passed out of death into life. **25** Most certainly I tell you, the hour comes, and now is, when the dead will hear the Son of God's voice; and those who hear will live. **26** For as the Father has life in himself, even so he gave to the Son also to have life in himself. **27** He also gave him authority to execute judgment, because he is a son of man. **28** Don't marvel at this, for the hour comes in which all who are in the tombs will hear his voice, **29** and will come out; those who have done good, to the resurrection of life; and those who have done evil, to the resurrection of judgment.

John 5:25-29 The Jews at this time were familiar with their ancestors hearing from prophets. Yet, God had stopped speaking to them for hundreds of years at this point (See note on John 4:25). When Jesus was speaking, he was speaking with the authority of a prophet – a man sent by God to deliver God's message. But, Jesus spoke with even more authority as He made claims that likened him directly to and with God.

👍 John 5:31-40 The first five books of the Bible are known as the Pentateuch. The fifth book is Deuteronomy, which is a compilation of sermons from Moses. According to this book, any matter could only be established as testimony if it had two or three witnesses. Because of this, Jesus's testimony of himself is not sufficient. Rather than rely on anyone else, such as John in verse 33, Jesus pointed to the works God had sent him to do, the works He actually did, His Heavenly Father, and the Scriptures as his witnesses.

John 5:33 When people have the same name, such as "John", it can be confusing. John, the writer of this Gospel, is not who Jesus is referring to here. He is speaking of John the Baptist. (See notes in John 1:19) The addition of "The Baptist" (or "The Baptizer") was done by those in the early church and passed on through the writings of the New Testament.

30 I can of myself do nothing. As I hear, I judge, and my judgment is righteous; because I don't seek my own will, but the will of my Father who sent me.

31 👍 "If I testify about myself, my witness is not valid. **32** It is another who testifies about me. I know that the testimony which he testifies about me is true. **33** You have sent to John, and he has testified to the truth. **34** But the testimony which I receive is not from man. However, I say these things that you may be saved. **35** He was the burning and shining lamp, and you were willing to rejoice for a while in his light. **36** But the testimony which I have is greater than that of John, for the works which the Father gave me to accomplish, the very works that I do, testify about me, that the Father has sent me. **37** The Father himself, who sent me, has testified about me. You have neither heard his voice at any time, nor seen his form. **38** You don't have his word living in you, because you don't believe him whom he sent.

39 "You search the ⌗Scriptures, because you think that in them you have eternal life; and these are they which testify about me. **40** Yet you will not come to me, that you may have life. **41** I don't receive glory from men. **42** But I know you, that you don't have God's love in yourselves. **43** I have come in my Father's name, and you don't receive me. If another comes in his own name, you will receive him. **44** How can you believe, who receive glory from one another, and you don't seek the glory that comes from the only God? 😠

45 "Don't think that I will accuse you to the Father. There is one who accuses you, even Moses, on whom you have set your hope. **46** For if you believed Moses, you would believe me; for he wrote about me. **47** But if you don't believe his writings, how will you believe my words?"

⌗ John 5:39 This verse talks about how the Scriptures point directly to Jesus. If you got eight things right about someone before they were ever born, mathematically that would be the same as if you would take silver dollars and stack them two feet tall over the entire state of Texas, put an "X" on one of the silver dollars, blindfold someone at the state border and sent them as far as they wanted into the state and they picked out just one silver dollar and it was the one that had the "X" on it. Picture that for a minute. Now, consider this: there are over 300 prophecies from the Old Testament that point directly to Jesus.

😠 John 5:44 Jesus, the master of asking questions, asks a very pointed one in this passage. Who or where are you seeking glory? Man? Or God? When Jesus's time has come, he will answer the question he poses here. (See note on John 17:4)

Introduction to Chapter 6

The book of John is full of signs and miracles. In Chapter 6 we see a miracle where Jesus meets the peoples' physical need of hunger. With just two loaves of bread and five fish, Jesus feeds a great multitude. 👍

How many?

The title in most Bibles is: "The feeding of the 5,000." We will learn it was way more than 5,000 that were fed that day. #️⃣

What we also see in this chapter is the popularity of Jesus growing. And it keeps growing. Jesus continues to meet other peoples' needs, even beyond their physical ones. 😌

Eventually, however, the crowds started to question. Then they started to complain. Finally, for many, following Jesus becomes too difficult. It comes with a cost that many are not willing to pay. 😕

Because of this, the crowds dwindle.

When this happens, Jesus addresses the twelve disciples that he chose. He wants to address their level of commitment. Peter, their outspoken leader, shares the faith they all have in Jesus as the Messiah.

At the end of the chapter, Jesus drops a bombshell about the twelve that not one of them could have ever seen coming. 😮

John 6:2 The miracles are starting to pile up in Jesus's favor, and his popularity is growing. He is showing evidence that he is the Messiah they have been looking and waiting for all these years. The Messiah brings hope for every generation with the promise of eternal life. Is this why the people followed Jesus, so that they might receive the eternal life promised to each of us? No. Sadly, the followed him because he could heal the sick, and they wanted to see more of this.

John 6:5-7 Another classic example of Jesus asking one question, and Philip answering his own thought going through his mind. Jesus asked "Where...?", and Philip answered with "what".

CHAPTER 6

After these things, Jesus went away to the other side of the sea of Galilee, which is also called the Sea of Tiberias. **2** A great multitude followed him, because they saw his signs which he did on those who were sick.

3 Jesus went up into the mountain, and he sat there with his disciples. **4** Now the Passover, the feast of the Jews, was at hand. **5** Jesus therefore lifting up his eyes, and seeing that a great multitude was coming to him, said to Philip, "Where are we to buy bread, that these may eat?" **6** He said this to test him, for he himself knew what he would do.

7 Philip answered him, "Two hundred denarii worth of bread is not sufficient for them, that every one of them may receive a little."

8 One of his disciples, Andrew, Simon Peter's brother, said to him, **9** "There is a boy here who has five barley loaves and two fish, but what are these among so many?"

10 Jesus said, "Have the people sit down." Now there was much grass in that place. So the men sat down, in number about five thousand. **11** Jesus took the loaves; and having given thanks, he distributed to the disciples, and the disciples to those who were sitting down; likewise also of the fish as much as they desired. **12** When they were filled, he said to his disciples, "Gather up the broken pieces which are left over, that nothing be lost." **13** So they gathered them up, and filled twelve baskets with broken pieces from the five barley loaves, which were left over by those who had eaten. **14** When therefore the people saw the sign which Jesus did, they said, "This is truly the prophet who comes into the world." **15** Jesus therefore, perceiving that they were about to come and take him by force to make him king , withdrew again to the mountain by himself.

John 6:10 This is the fourth miracle (sign) recorded in the Gospel of John. It is titled "The Feeding of the 5,000" in many Bibles. However, if you notice in the verse, it says there were 5,000 *men*. If 60% of those men were married, that would be add 3,000 women to the total. If they averaged a child per household, that is another 3,000 kids. In other words, there could have easily been over 10,000 people fed that day!

John 6:15 The people were in need of someone to deliver them from the Roman's who were in power. If this man could feed thousands in need in an instant, He must be able to break the chains of their bondage from the Romans. Because of the sign that Jesus performed, they wanted to make Him their earthly king. Jesus wanted nothing to do with this temporary title; He wanted them to see his Heavenly Father.

John 6:19 A "stadia" is a little over 600 feet. So the disciples had rowed 15,000-18,000 feet. This is equivalent to three miles or more in modern terms.

John 6:20 Notice that Jesus didn't say "It's me, Jesus." He said "It is I." The disciples would understand this as "I AM", referring directly to God, from their readings of the Scriptures. (See note on John 6:35)

John 6:20 The term "do not be afraid" appears in the Bible 365 times. It is a daily reminder that when God is with us, there is no need to fear!

16 When evening came, his disciples went down to the sea. **17** They entered into the boat, and were going over the sea to Capernaum. It was now dark, and Jesus had not come to them. **18** The sea was tossed by a great wind blowing. **19** When therefore they had rowed about twenty-five or thirty stadia , they saw Jesus walking on the sea, and drawing near to the boat; and they were afraid. **20** But he said to them, "It is I. Don't be afraid." **21** They were willing therefore to receive him into the boat. Immediately the boat was at the land where they were going.

22 On the next day, the multitude that stood on the other side of the sea saw that there was no other boat there, except the one in which his disciples had embarked, and that Jesus hadn't entered with his disciples into the boat, but his disciples had gone away alone.

23 However boats from Tiberias came near to the place where they ate the bread after the Lord had given thanks. 24 When the multitude therefore saw that Jesus wasn't there, nor his disciples, they themselves got into the boats, and came to Capernaum, seeking Jesus. 25 When they found him on the other side of the sea, they asked him, "Rabbi, when did you come here?" 26 Jesus answered them, 😮 "Most certainly I tell you, you seek me, not because you saw signs, but because you ate of the loaves, and were filled. 27 Don't work for the food which perishes, but for the food which remains to eternal life, which the Son of Man will give to you. For God the Father has sealed him."

28 They said therefore to him, 😐 "What must we do, that we may work the works of God?"

29 Jesus answered them, "This is the work of God, that you believe in him whom he has sent."

😮 John 6:26 -27 Jesus didn't sugarcoat his words here. He knew the motives of the people seeking Him. They were focused on the here and now and were both selfish and self-centered. Fill me first physically, and then I will follow you spiritually was their thought process. Follow me spiritually, and you will be filled physically, was what Jesus was trying to teach them. It is the same message for us today.

😐 John 6:28-29 A question that people are often asked and even ask of themselves is what should I do with my life? This question often centers on the work that they would do, meaning their occupation. This could mean pursuing an education, serving in the military, perfecting a trade, or full time ministry. For the believer, the question then is the same as it is now: how does the work that I do reflect the work of God in my life? Jesus answers this question for us in these verses: believe in the one that God sent and your work can't help but reflect Jesus.

👍 John 6:32-33 There are two breads being discussed here. The first is "manna" which was the bread God, not Moses as Jesus notes here, sent from Heaven to feed the Israelites on their journey to the Promised Land. The second is the bread of life, which God also sent in the form of Jesus.

\# John 6:35 This is the first of seven statements that Jesus states and defines "I AM". This comes from the discussion God had with Moses and Moses asked God who he should say is leading them into the Promised Land. God said, "I AM". The seven times in John that Jesus said, "I AM" are (see notes on each): John 6:35 (passage through verse 51; John 8:12 (tied to John 9:5); John 10:7-10; John 10:11-14; John 11:25; John 14:6; John 15:1) *NOTE: See also note on John 8:58.*

John 6:35 The Israelites were given manna, which was bread from heaven, to feed them physically as they wandered across the desert. Jesus fills us spiritually and feeds us where we are empty every day as he states, "I am the bread of life."

30 They said therefore to him, "What then do you do for a sign, that we may see and believe you? What work do you do? **31** Our fathers ate the manna in the wilderness. As it is written, 'He gave them bread out of heaven to eat.' "

32 Jesus therefore said to them, "Most certainly, I tell you, it wasn't Moses who gave you the bread out of heaven, but my Father gives you the true bread out of heaven. 👍 **33** For the bread of God is that which comes down out of heaven, and gives life to the world."

34 They said therefore to him, "Lord, always give us this bread."

35 Jesus said to them, "I am \# the bread of life. Whoever comes to me will not be hungry, and whoever believes in me will never be thirsty. **36** But I told you that you have seen me, and yet you don't believe. **37** All those whom the Father gives me will come to me. He who comes to me I will in no way throw out.

38 For I have come down from heaven, not to do my own will, but the will of him who sent me. **39** This is the will of my Father who sent me, that of all he has given to me I should lose nothing, but should raise him up at the last day. **40** This is the will of the one who sent me, that everyone who sees the Son, and believes in him, should have eternal life; and I will raise him up at the last day."

41 The Jews therefore murmured concerning him, because he said, "I am the bread which came down out of heaven." **42** They said, "Isn't this Jesus, the son of Joseph, whose father and mother we know? How then does he say, 'I have come down out of heaven?' "

43 Therefore Jesus answered them, "Don't murmur among yourselves. **44** No one can come to me unless the Father who sent me draws him, and I will raise him up in the last day.

John 6:38-40 Here we see the process of salvation, in Jesus's words. God sent us Jesus (Jesus came to us verse 38) and for all of those that come to him (believe in him, verse 40), will live forever (eternal life, verse 40), even though they have to die first, physically (raise him up at the last day, verse 40).

John 6:41-43 When God gave manna to the people on their journey to the Promised Land, what did they do? The same thing they did here when the Bread of Life was given to them: they murmured and they questioned. (Read Exodus 15:24)

John 6:48-51 In every culture there is one common staple you will find that is on virtually every dinner table: bread. Think about where bread came from. It started as a seed that was planted, grew, was cut down, ground up and crushed, and thrown in the fire. After it is baked is when we enjoy it. The same can be said about Jesus, as the bread of life.

John 6:49-51 Notice the difference that Jesus points out here. Those that ate bread in the wilderness died. Those that accept Jesus as the bread of life will not die. In fact, they will live forever.

45 It is written in the prophets, 'They will all be taught by God.' Therefore everyone who hears from the Father and has learned, comes to me. **46** Not that anyone has seen the Father, except he who is from God. He has seen the Father. **47** Most certainly, I tell you, he who believes in me has eternal life. **48** I am the bread of life. **49** Your fathers ate the manna in the wilderness and they died. **50** This is the bread which comes down out of heaven, that anyone may eat of it and not die. **51** I am the living bread which came down out of heaven. If anyone eats of this bread, he will live forever. Yes, the bread which I will give for the life of the world is my flesh."

52 The Jews therefore contended with one another, saying, "How can this man give us his flesh to eat?"

53 Jesus therefore said to them, "Most certainly I tell you, unless you eat the flesh of the Son of Man and drink his blood, you don't have life in

yourselves. **54** He who eats my flesh and drinks my blood has eternal life,
and I will raise him up at the last day. **55** For my flesh is food indeed, and my blood is drink indeed. **56** He who eats my flesh and drinks my blood lives in me, and I in him. **57** As the living Father sent me, and I live because of the Father; so he who feeds on me, he will also live because of me. **58** This is the bread which came down out of heaven—not as our fathers ate the manna, and died. He who eats this bread will live forever." **59** He said these things in the synagogue, as he taught in Capernaum.

60 Therefore many of his disciples, when they heard this, said, "This is a hard saying! Who can listen to it?"

61 But Jesus knowing in himself that his disciples murmured at this, said to them, "Does this cause you to stumble? **62** Then what if you would see the Son of Man ascending to where he was before?

50

John 6:54-56 This may be confusing to people now, but you have to consider the culture at this time. Jesus isn't talking about being a cannibal here. He is talking about consuming (eating and drinking) the Word of God and its meaning. He explains this further in John 6:63 when He says: "The words that I speak to you are spirit and life."

John 6:60-66 Ministry is difficult. Make no mistake about it. Why? Those in ministry have to deal with people, who are flawed. Not everybody liked or loved Jesus. Following rules was easy. Following Jesus made people stop and ask themselves if it was worth it. In the end, many gave up and left, going their own way. Many people today still do the same.

John 6:67-69 Jesus asked the disciples a question. This time, Peter actually answered the question that Jesus asked. His answer was not just for him, it was for the entire group of twelve. It may be the best answer Peter ever gave to any question! The disciples understood that Jesus's words were eternal. They also believed he was the Anointed One –the Christ – and God's very own Son!

John 6:70-71 Here we see that Jesus admits he knew what he was doing when he chose Judas as one of the 12 disciples. No, Jesus didn't make a mistake. His choice fulfilled a prophecy about Jesus specifically (Psalm 41:9). Even after Judas betrayed Jesus, Jesus still called him "friend" until the very end (Matthew 26:50). As for Judas? Even he admitted that Jesus did nothing wrong (Matthew 27:4). He threw his reward back to the ones who paid for the information on Jesus. They used that same blood money to purchase a field to bury people in when they died.

63 It is the spirit who gives life. The flesh profits nothing. The words that I speak to you are spirit, and are life. **64** But there are some of you who don't believe." For Jesus knew from the beginning who they were who didn't believe, and who it was who would betray him. **65** He said, "For this cause I have said to you that no one can come to me, unless it is given to him by my Father." **66** At this, many of his disciples went back, and walked no more with him. **67** Jesus said therefore to the twelve, "You don't also want to go away, do you?" **68** Simon Peter answered him, "Lord, to whom would we go? You have the words of eternal life. **69** We have come to believe and know that you are the Christ, the Son of the living God."

70 Jesus answered them, "Didn't I choose you, the twelve, and one of you is a devil?" **71**Now he spoke of Judas Iscariot, for it was he who would betray him, being one of the twelve.

Introduction to Chapter 7

Some people think that Jesus was an only child. In this chapter we see this was not the case as his own brothers tried to tempt Jesus to do things he shouldn't.

Sadly, even his own brothers did not believe in Him. (That will change in time as the books of James and Jude were written by the half brothers of Jesus. They didn't understand and believe in Jesus until His resurrection.)

On top of his own family being in disbelief, the Pharisees were doing whatever they could to trick and trap Jesus. It was not working, as Jesus said throughout the book of John, "My hour has not yet come".

The Jews were torn about Jesus. Some believed him to be the Christ. Others questioned this based on where they believed him to be from and who his relatives were. Still others marveled at his teaching, acknowledging that he wasn't an educated man.

The further we read the chapter, the more intense it becomes. Toward the end, confusion has set in, as the people argued over who Jesus was, when the chapter suddenly ends...

Remember that this was a letter written for everyone to read. When it was translated for us to read today, verses and chapters were inserted for each of us to break down the written Word and for it to be the same, regardless of the version you read.

John 7:2 There are Seven Feasts of Israel (or the Jews) that were celebrated each year: Passover, Unleavened Bread, First Fruits, Pentecost, Trumpets, Atonement, and Tabernacles. The Feast of the Tabernacles was also known as the Feast of the Booths. Devout Jews would build small huts outside of their homes and worship Him there. It is celebrated as a reminder that God provided shelter when they walked through the wilderness and desert.

John 7:5 (Look back at the note on John 2:12.) We often think of Jesus as being an only child. But, he had brothers and/or sisters like many of us do!

John 7:8 This is the second time that Jesus shared that it wasn't his time yet. He will share this two more times in this Gospel. Know this, though: Jesus's time is coming. (See note on John 2:4)

CHAPTER 7

After these things, Jesus was walking in Galilee, for he wouldn't walk in Judea, because the Jews sought to kill him. **2** Now the feast of the Jews, the Feast of Booths, was at hand. **3** His brothers therefore said to him, "Depart from here and go into Judea, that your disciples also may see your works which you do. **4** For no one does anything in secret while he seeks to be known openly. If you do these things, reveal yourself to the world." **5** For even his brothers didn't believe in him.

6 Jesus therefore said to them, "My time has not yet come, but your time is always ready. **7** The world can't hate you, but it hates me, because I testify about it, that its works are evil. **8** You go up to the feast. I am not yet going up to this feast, because my time is not yet fulfilled."

⁹ Having said these things to them, he stayed in Galilee. ¹⁰ But when his brothers had gone up to the feast, then he also went up, not publicly, but as it were in secret. ¹¹ The Jews therefore sought him at the feast, and said, "Where is he?" ¹² There was much murmuring among the multitudes concerning him. Some said, "He is a good man." Others said, "Not so, but he leads the multitude astray." ¹³ Yet no one spoke openly of him for fear of the Jews. ¹⁴ But when it was now the middle of the feast, Jesus went up into the temple and taught. ¹⁵ The Jews therefore marveled, saying, "How does this man know letters, having never been educated?" ¹⁶ Jesus therefore answered them, "My teaching is not mine, but his who sent me. ¹⁷ If anyone desires to do his will, he will know about the teaching, whether it is from God, or if I am speaking from myself.

John 7:14-15 It was the Jews that marveled when Jesus taught. His message was one of love, and they were used to the book being taught as the law. We all use excuses to not learn and teach God's word: we are too old or too young, we don't know enough, we don't have the education, etc. Jesus showed us that if we love others as God loves us, our formal education doesn't matter. Our willingness to love others does.

John 7:16 How do you look at God's word? Is it a book of rules and regulations? Is it the law? Maybe you see it as a love letter? Jesus gave us some insight that we may not have considered. His words were not only meant to show God's love, but they were meant to teach us. It was up to those who read and listened to choose, or to refuse, to learn from those words.

John 7:19-20 The people listening were very aware of the law Moses gave to their relatives many years ago. One of the Ten Commandments was "Thou Shalt Not Kill". These words were both true and painful to those listening.

John 7:20 People still were not sure what it was they believed about Jesus. Was he the Messiah that everyone had been looking and waiting for all this time? Or, did he have something seriously wrong with him? Remember, also, at this time, that the people didn't realize there was a plot to kill Jesus (See note on John 5:18). This man that healed the sick, gave vision to the blind, made those that were paralyzed walk, and even raised people from the dead must have something wrong with him since he didn't have an army to take over and be the power they all expected. Instead, Jesus just loved others and did what God would do: give and share life. God won't force himself on anyone. Love doesn't need to (Read 1 Corinthians 13:4-8a) as, in the end, it will never fail.

18 He who speaks from himself seeks his own glory, but he who seeks the glory of him who sent him is true, and no unrighteousness is in him. **19** Didn't Moses give you the law, and yet none of you keeps the law? Why do you seek to kill me?"

20 The multitude answered, "You have a demon! Who seeks to kill you?"

21 Jesus answered them, "I did one work and you all marvel because of it. **22** Moses has given you circumcision (not that it is of Moses, but of the fathers), and on the Sabbath you circumcise a boy. **23** If a boy receives circumcision on the Sabbath, that the law of Moses may not be broken, are you angry with me, because I made a man completely healthy on the Sabbath? **24** Don't judge according to appearance, but judge righteous judgment."

25 Therefore some of them of Jerusalem said, "Isn't this he whom they seek to kill?

²⁶ Behold, he speaks openly, and they say nothing to him. Can it be that the rulers indeed know that this is truly the Christ?

²⁷ However we know where this man comes from, but when the Christ comes, no one will know where he comes from." ²⁸ Jesus therefore cried out in the temple, teaching and saying, "You both know me, and know where I am from. I have not come of myself, but he who sent me is true, whom you don't know. ²⁹ I know him, because I am from him, and he sent me."

³⁰ They sought therefore to take him; but no one laid a hand on him, because his hour had not yet come. ³¹ But of the multitude, many believed in him. They said, "When the Christ comes, he won't do more signs than those which this man has done, will he?" ³² The Pharisees heard the multitude murmuring these things concerning him, and the chief priests and the Pharisees sent officers to arrest him.

John 7:26-27 Many generations had died looking for the Christ, meaning "The Anointed One" (See notes on John 1:25, John 6:67-69, and John 12:34). Suddenly, this man before them spoke as the one they had been looking to find for so many years. Their relatives and ancestors had missed Him. Yet He was now in their presence. They didn't want to miss Him. But, they still couldn't come to the reality that this carpenter's son from Nazareth could be their Messiah, their savior.

John 7:30-34 We are now in the midst of the greatest story ever told. It is also the greatest story ever known: a story about a man that was sent by God to save a world that needed a savior. Some believed. Others did not. In the center of the story wasn't just a man named Jesus, it was God Himself. Jesus was the kindest, most caring, wisest, loving, and most powerful man to ever walk the Earth.

John 7:35 The "Dispersion" was referring to the Jews that had been scattered throughout the world over time, in this case Greece. The term "Greeks" also included Gentiles. The Jews were asking if Jesus was going out to teach anyone that wasn't in Jerusalem. Jerusalem was their city, with protective walls around it, and they were not about to chase Jesus outside of it for any reason.

John 7:40 "The prophet" the multitude was referring to was the Messiah. The "Messiah" was the one that would deliver, lead, and save people from the ones who were in power. The Messiah wouldn't use His power to save them, as the people expected, rather, in Jesus, it would be God's love that would deliver each of them. In the end, they missed God, his message through his son Jesus, and, eventually, eternal life through God's Holy Spirit.

33 Then Jesus said, "I will be with you a little while longer, then I go to him who sent me. **34** You will seek me, and won't find me. You can't come where I am."
35 The Jews therefore said among themselves, "Where will this man go that we won't find him? Will he go to the Dispersion among the Greeks, and teach the Greeks? **36** What is this word that he said, 'You will seek me, and won't find me;' and 'Where I am, you can't come'?"

37 Now on the last and greatest day of the feast, Jesus stood and cried out, "If anyone is thirsty, let him come to me and drink! **38** He who believes in me, as the Scripture has said, from within him will flow rivers of living water." **39** But he said this about the Spirit, which those believing in him were to receive. For the Holy Spirit was not yet given, because Jesus wasn't yet glorified.

40 Many of the multitude therefore, when they heard these words, said, "This is truly the prophet."

41 Others said, "This is the Christ." But some said, "What, does the Christ come out of Galilee? **42** Hasn't the Scripture said that the Christ comes of the offspring of David, and from Bethlehem 👍, the village where David was?" **43** So a division arose in the multitude because of him. **44** Some of them would have arrested him, but no one laid hands on him. **45** The officers therefore came to the chief priests and Pharisees, and they said to them, "Why didn't you bring him?"

46 The officers answered, "No man ever spoke like this man!"

47 The Pharisees therefore answered them, "You aren't also led astray, are you? **48** Have any of the rulers believed in him, or of the Pharisees? **49** But this multitude that doesn't know the law is cursed."

50 Nicodemus (he who came to him by night, being one of them) said to them, **51** "Does our law judge a man, unless it first hears from him personally and knows what he does?"

👍 John 7:42 There are many towns named Bethlehem in the area that Jesus lived. This Bethlehem was the specific town that was described over 700 years before the book of John was written as referenced in the book of Micah 5:2.

John 7:46 Up to this point in history, and after this point in history, every major power had been built with force. When the officers heard Jesus speak, they realized he was building something never before (and never since) seen: he was building on love. Why? Because God is love (1 John 4:8)

John 7:50-52 Nicodemus, who Jesus shared the second most quoted verse in the Bible in John 3:16 (see note) talked to the Pharisees with what they knew best: the law. The Pharisees turned on this well-educated, highly respected person who happened to be a part of their religious group, because of their hatred of Jesus.

John 7:52 The Pharisees are supposed to know everything there is about Scripture. Yet, in this verse they show that they know what they want to know. There were five prophets from Galilee, as opposed to the zero that they claimed here: Jonah, Nahum, Hosea, Elijah, and Elisha.

52 They answered him, "Are you also from Galilee? Search, and see that no prophet has arisen out of Galilee."

53 Everyone went to his own house,

Introduction to Chapter 8

This chapter starts with one of the most intense exchanges in the Bible. Jesus was about to teach in the temple when the Pharisees brought in a woman caught in adultery. 👀 Notice they didn't bring in a woman and a man. They just brought in the woman. A woman was a second-class citizen in this culture. After all, it was the woman that brought sin into the world. (Read Genesis 3 closely and you will see that sin didn't enter the world until Adam also ate of the fruit and that Adam was with Eve and he did nothing to stop her. 😮)

The law states they needed to stone the woman. They asked Jesus what they should do, even though they knew the law.

Jesus's response to them gives us so much insight into the very God we serve. His response shows us the character of the God that created each of us. His response shows us the compassion of the God that calls each one of us His children. 😕

Then, the very next response Jesus gave was to the woman caught in this terrible sin. He couldn't address the man who was part of the same sin, as he wasn't there. But Jesus's remark would have been the same to the man, just as it would be to each of us.

What was that response?

Read on to learn what it was!

CHAPTER 8

John 8:1 Doesn't it seem odd that the first verse of Chapter 8 isn't at the beginning of a sentence? Not all versions are like this. Some end chapter 7 with a sentence and start chapter 8 with a new sentence. Some do not. Don't allow a punctuation mark or a capital letter stop you from reading God's love letter to you! This was a letter written to each of us. The chapters and verses were added when the words were translated from the original languages into English.

John 8:6 What did Jesus write on the ground? Is this evidence of the first text message? Did he draw a line to dare the Pharisees to cross it? Or was he just gathering his thoughts and being quick to listen and slow to speak as the Bible teaches (James 1:19). The fact is, we do not know. We do know what happens next after this act. Read on!

but Jesus went to the Mount of Olives. ² Now very early in the morning, he came again into the temple, and all the people came to him. He sat down and taught them. ³ The scribes and the Pharisees brought a woman taken in adultery. Having set her in the middle, ⁴ they told him, "Teacher, we found this woman in adultery, in the very act. ⁵ Now in our law, Moses commanded us to stone such women. What then do you say about her?" ⁶ They said this testing him, that they might have something to accuse him of.

But Jesus stooped down and wrote on the ground with his finger. ⁷ But when they continued asking him, he looked up and said to them, "He who is without sin among you, let him throw the first stone at her." ⁸ Again he stooped down and wrote on the ground with his finger.

9 They, when they heard it 👍 , being convicted by their conscience, went out one by one, beginning from the oldest #️⃣ , even to the last. Jesus was left alone with the woman where she was, in the middle. **10** Jesus, standing up, saw her and said, "Woman, where are your accusers? Did no one condemn you?"

11 She said, "No one, Lord."

Jesus said, "Neither do I condemn you. Go your way. From now on, sin no more."

12 Again, therefore, Jesus spoke to them, saying, "I am the light of the world. He who follows me will not walk in the darkness, but will have the light of life." **13** The Pharisees therefore said to him, "You testify about yourself. Your testimony is not valid." **14** Jesus answered them, "Even if I testify about myself, my testimony is true, for I know where I came from, and where I am going; but you don't know where I came from, or where I am going.

👍 John 8:7-9 Notice it wasn't what Jesus wrote that was important. It was the words He spoke. Jesus didn't list all of the things they did wrong. He didn't point an accusing finger. He simply said something that they heard that made them think. After hearing the words, and thinking things through, each of them made their decision on how to deal with this woman.

#️⃣ John 8:9 Why start with the oldest? In virtually any culture, the older you are, the more wisdom you should have attained. The writer was saying that the wisest person, who was the oldest in age, left the woman alone, and individually – one by one – the others all followed until it was just Jesus and the woman.

John 8:20 The treasury in the temple was also known as "The Court of Women". This didn't mean that only women could enter, it meant that this court was as far as women could go into the temple.

John 8:20 Jesus's hour had not yet come. (See note on John 2...) The conversations are starting to focus on Jesus and his Father in heaven, which will give the Pharisees the ammunition they need to arrest him and his charge: blasphemy. Know this: tension is mounting, and Jesus's hour is approaching.

¹⁵ You judge according to the flesh. I judge no one. ¹⁶ Even if I do judge, my judgment is true, for I am not alone, but I am with the Father who sent me. ¹⁷ It's also written in your law that the testimony of two people is valid. ¹⁸ I am one who testifies about myself, and the Father who sent me testifies about me."

¹⁹ They said therefore to him, "Where is your Father?"

Jesus answered, "You know neither me nor my Father. If you knew me, you would know my Father also." ²⁰ Jesus spoke these words in the treasury, as he taught in the temple. Yet no one arrested him, because his hour had not yet come. ²¹ Jesus said therefore again to them, "I am going away, and you will seek me, and you will die in your sins. Where I go, you can't come."

²² The Jews therefore said, "Will he kill himself, because he says, 'Where I am going, you can't come'?"

²³ He said to them, "You are from beneath. I am from above. You are of this world. I am not of this world. ²⁴ I said therefore to you that you will die in your sins; for unless you believe that I am he, you will die in your sins."

²⁵ They said therefore to him, "Who are you?"
Jesus said to them, "Just what I have been saying to you from the beginning. ²⁶ I have many things to speak and to judge concerning you. However he who sent me is true; and
the things which I heard from him, these I say to the world."

²⁷ They didn't understand that he spoke to them about the Father. ²⁸ Jesus therefore said to them, "When you have lifted up the Son of Man, then you will know that I am he, and I do nothing of myself, but as my Father taught me, I say these things.

John 8:22 The Pharisees are not asking if Jesus is going to take his own life and commit suicide. They are mocking him at this point. They know that death would be one place that they could no longer grab ahold of him and arrest or beat him.

John 8:28 This is one of the 83 times in the four gospels (Matthew, Mark, Luke, and John) that the term "Son of Man" was used to identify Jesus.

John 8:28 Jesus was giving the Jews a sign of the things to come. The Jews "lifting up the Son of Man" was the picture of them putting Jesus up on the cross.

John 8:34-35 The Jews were confusing what true freedom was. They thought it was about the political party that held power over them. At this time, that was the Romans. Jesus was trying to help them understand that what held power over them was what controlled each of them individually. That was sin. Sin was and is "missing the mark". So when we sin, we miss the mark with God. In this case, what controlled them personally caused them to miss God eternally. It held them back from living a life focused on God. This is the same thing that can happen to each one of us still to this day.

29 He who sent me is with me. The Father hasn't left me alone, for I always do the things that are pleasing to him."

30 As he spoke these things, many believed in him. **31** Jesus therefore said to those Jews who had believed him, "If you remain in my word, then you are truly my disciples. **32** You will know the truth, and the truth will make you free."

33 They answered him, "We are Abraham's offspring, and have never been in bondage to anyone. How do you say, 'You will be made free'?"

34 Jesus answered them, "Most certainly I tell you, everyone who commits sin is the bondservant of sin. **35** A bondservant doesn't live in the house forever. A son remains forever. **36** If therefore the Son makes you free, you will be free indeed. **37** I know that you are Abraham's offspring, yet you seek to kill me, because my word finds no place in you.

38 I say the things which I have seen with my Father; and you also do the things which you have seen with your father."

39 They answered him, "Our father is Abraham." Jesus said to them, "If you were Abraham's children, you would do the works of Abraham. **40** But now you seek to kill me, a man who has told you the truth which I heard from God. Abraham didn't do this. **41** You do the works of your father."

They said to him, "We were not born of sexual immorality. We have one Father, God."

42 Therefore Jesus said to them, "If God were your father, you would love 🔳 me, for I came out and have come from God. For I haven't come of myself, but he sent me. **43** Why don't you understand my speech? Because you can't hear my word. **44** You are of your father, the devil, and you want to do the desires of your father. He was a murderer from the beginning, and doesn't stand in the truth, because there is no truth in him. When he speaks a

John 8:41 Abraham was the father of many nations, and considered the first chosen person of the chosen people, the Jews (Genesis 17). Jesus pointed out that if these people did as Abraham would have done, they wouldn't seek to kill Him. Therefore, their father would be Satan himself, who seeks to steal, kill, and destroy (See John 10:10 with note).

John 8:42 A central theme in the gospel of John is love. It shows up nearly 50 times in his gospel. Remember, John was described as the disciple Jesus loved. We don't think about Jesus having emotions (See notes on Lazarus in John 11) or feelings or even friends, but he had to, as he was both God and man.

John 8:47 Jesus is teaching one of the best lessons any person can learn. People (including you and I) don't listen so they can understand and grow. Instead, we listen to reply. Be very aware of this. If you listen to reply, how can you ever hear God speaking to you so that you can understand what he can do in (and for) your life?

John 8:48 The Jews hated the Samaritans. When they called Jesus a Samaritan this was the worst name a Jew could call him. That wasn't enough for the Jews, though. They added that he must also have a demon.

lie, he speaks on his own; for he is a liar, and the father of lies. **45** But because I tell the truth, you don't believe me. **46** Which of you convicts me of sin? If I tell the truth, why do you not believe me? **47** He who is of God hears the words of God. For this cause you don't hear, because you are not of God."

48 Then the Jews answered him, "Don't we say well that you are a Samaritan , and have a demon?"

49 Jesus answered, "I don't have a demon, but I honor my Father and you dishonor me. **50** But I don't seek my own glory. There is one who seeks and judges. **51** Most certainly, I tell you, if a person keeps my word, he will never see death."

52 Then the Jews said to him, "Now we know that you have a demon. Abraham died, as did the prophets; and you say, 'If a man keeps my word, he will never taste of death.'

53 Are you greater than our father, Abraham, who died? The prophets died. Who do you make yourself out to be?" **54** Jesus answered, "If I glorify myself, my glory is nothing. It is my Father who glorifies me, of whom you say that he is our God. **55** You have not known him, but I know him. If I said, 'I don't know him,' I would be like you, a liar. But I know him and keep his word. **56** Your father Abraham rejoiced to see my day. He saw it, and was glad."

57 The Jews therefore said to him, "You are not yet fifty years old! Have you seen Abraham?"

58 Jesus said to them, "Most certainly, I tell you, before Abraham came into existence, I AM."

59 Therefore they took up stones to throw at him, but Jesus was hidden, and went out of the temple, having gone through the middle of them, and so passed by.

John 8:58 This is not considered one of Jesus's "I Am..." statements as Jesus does not define it. The "I AM" Jesus refers to in this verse is God and God alone. (See note on John 6:35 for the first "I Am..." statement with the list and location of the other six in the Gospel of John).

John 8:59 The Jews were so angry they wanted to kill Jesus. Jesus was able to go right through all of them and they couldn't see Him. Why? As He shared multiple times in this gospel (See note on John 2:4), it was not yet His time.

Introduction to Chapter 9

The chapter starts with a miracle that had never been heard of to this point in history. A man that was born blind was given his sight. Of course, it was Jesus who performed the miracle. And, of course, the Pharisees, the religious rule makers, didn't want to believe that it was Jesus that had done such a thing. Just as had happened to the man that was paralyzed for 38 years, Jesus performed this miracle on the Sabbath.

In typical Pharisee style, they questioned the man who could now see, who gave credit to Jesus. Giving any credit to Jesus now had a punishment, and that was being thrown out of the temple. But the Pharisees wanted to make sure this man was truly blind from birth, so they questioned his parents, too. The parents, out of fear of being thrown out of the temple, confirmed that their son was blind from birth, but also told the Pharisees he was of age and to talk to him about what had taken place.

The Pharisees did just that. The two had an exchange and the formerly blind man told the Pharisees that what he knew for sure was that "though I was blind, now I see". The exchange continued and, eventually, the Pharisees threw the man out of the temple.

Jesus found the same man, and they had a discussion, as well. In the end, the man saw Jesus for who He was, the Son of God, and believed. Jesus finished with a conversation about this subject with the Pharisees.

How did that end? Read on, you just have to see!

John 9:3 Here we get to see a theme that was typical in this time and culture: the blame game. If someone had a sickness, were unable to have babies, broke a bone, wasn't chosen, etc. it was always someone else's fault. Since this man couldn't see, it obviously had to be something that he or his family had done. People were always looking for the sin in other people's lives. Jesus pointed out that being blind (or sick, or barren, or hurt, etc.) wasn't anyone's fault if it wasn't done intentionally. Instead of looking at what this person did wrong, look to see what God could do through this person's life in this area that wasn't normal.

CHAPTER 9

As he passed by, he saw a man blind from birth. **2** His disciples asked him, "Rabbi, who sinned, this man or his parents, that he was born blind?"

3 Jesus answered, "This man didn't sin, nor did his parents; but, that the works of God might be revealed in him. **4** I must work the works of him who sent me while it is day. The night is coming, when no one can work. **5** While I am in the world, I am the light of the world." **6** When he had said this, he spat on the ground, made mud with the saliva, anointed the blind man's eyes with the mud, **7** and said to him, "Go, wash in the pool of Siloam" (which means "Sent"). So he went away, washed, and came back seeing. **8** The neighbors therefore, and those who saw that he was blind before, said, "Isn't this he who sat and begged?" **9** Others were saying, "It is he." Still others were saying, "He looks like him."

He said, "I am he." **10** They therefore were asking him, "How were your eyes opened?"

11 He answered, "A man called Jesus made mud, anointed my eyes, and said to me, 'Go to the pool of Siloam and wash.' So I went away and washed, and I received sight."

12 Then they asked him, "Where is he?"

He said, "I don't know."

13 They brought him who had been blind to the Pharisees. 👍

14 It was a Sabbath when Jesus made the mud and opened his eyes. 😐 **15** Again therefore the Pharisees also asked him how he received his sight. He said to them, "He put mud on my eyes, I washed, and I see."

16 Some therefore of the Pharisees said, "This man is not from God, because he doesn't keep the Sabbath." Others said, "How can a man who is a sinner do such signs?" So there was division among them. **17** Therefore they asked the blind man again, "What do you

👍 John 9:13 Who made the rules? The Pharisees did. Who had to listen to the rules? The Jews did. Is there an easy way to remember that the Pharisees decided what was right or wrong, regardless of whether it was popular? Yes, there is. Most people didn't like the rules they made and how it affected every day lives: I didn't like that rule, it wasn't right. In other words, it wasn't Fair-I-See.

😐 John 9:13-14 The hostility toward Jesus was growing. Why? Once again, because of what was happening in this time and place. You and I see Jesus healing a man that had been blind his entire life. The religious people of the day, the Pharisees, saw Jesus working on the Sabbath. The Sabbath was the Holy Day of the week. No one worked on the Sabbath.

John 9:17 The Pharisees couldn't bring themselves to believe in Jesus. They even asked the man that was now able to see what he thought, and he made his statement that "Jesus is a prophet." The Jews hadn't heard from a prophet in 400 years. This was a sign. It should have been seen as a sign from God. But, because of their jealousy, the Pharisees just couldn't bring themselves to a place of belief.

John 9:18-23 Another sign of the times. The parents of this man that was blind since birth were so fearful of the Jews, that they couldn't even be excited for their son and his newly given vision. Rather than share in their excitement, they were more worried about their place in the synagogue (this is comparable to our modern day church) than the amazing work that God had done.

say about him, because he opened your eyes?" He said, "He is a prophet."

18 The Jews therefore didn't believe concerning him, that he had been blind, and had received his sight, until they called the parents of him who had received his sight, **19** and asked them, "Is this your son, whom you say was born blind? How then does he now see?"

20 His parents answered them, "We know that this is our son, and that he was born blind; **21** but how he now sees, we don't know; or who opened his eyes, we don't know. He is of age. Ask him. He will speak for himself." **22** His parents said these things because they feared the Jews; for the Jews had already agreed that if any man would confess him as Christ, he would be put out of the synagogue. **23** Therefore his parents said, "He is of age. Ask him." **24** So they called the man who was blind a second time, and said to him, "Give glory to God. We know that this man is a sinner."

²⁵ He therefore answered, "I don't know if he is a sinner. One thing I do know: that though I was blind, now I see."
²⁶ They said to him again, "What did he do to you? How did he open your eyes?" ²⁷ He answered them, "I told you already, and you didn't listen. Why do you want to hear it again? 👍 You don't also want to become his disciples, do you?"

²⁸ They insulted him and said, "You are his disciple, but we are disciples of Moses. ²⁹ We know that God has spoken to Moses. But as for this man, we don't know where he comes from."

³⁰ The man answered them, "How amazing! You don't know where he comes from, yet he opened my eyes. ³¹ We know that God doesn't listen to sinners, but if anyone is a worshiper of God, and does his will, he listens to him. ³² 🔲 Since the world began it has never been heard of that anyone opened the eyes of someone born blind. ³³ If this man were not from God, he could do nothing." 😕

👍 John 9:27 One of the best exchanges in the Bible, between the Pharisees and this man whose name is never revealed, and also one of the most telling: the Pharisees didn't really want to listen to *what* Jesus had done. They, once again, just wanted to find *fault* in what He had done. (See notes on John 9:1 and 9:13)

🔲 John 9:30-32 The man that couldn't see directed the religious leaders to the one that opened his eyes. And, as he also pointed out, when has this been done before to someone who was born blind? In the history of the world to that date: exactly zero times. Never. Nada. Zilch. Who else would you point to in a time like this, but God?

😕 John 9:33 The man that could now see gave a very logical reason behind his newfound sight. He didn't credit magic, illusions, or a medical miracle. Instead he pointed to the only source that made any sense at all, and one that everyone there should have willingly embraced: God.

John 9:34 The formerly blind man had been listening his whole life. Now that he can finally see, he couldn't believe his ears. What did the Pharisees do when they heard these words that they didn't want to hear? They got rid of him. That just doesn't seem Fair-I-See. (See note on John 9:13.)

John 9:39 Does this sound familiar? It should: "I once was lost but now I'm found, was blind, but now, I see." That's Amazing Grace! (See note on how to remember G.R.A.C.E. in John 1:16)

34 They answered him, "You were altogether born in sins, and do you teach us?" Then they threw him out.

35 Jesus heard that they had thrown him out, and finding him, he said, "Do you believe in the Son of God?"

36 He answered, "Who is he, Lord, that I may believe in him?"

37 Jesus said to him, "You have both seen him, and it is he who speaks with you."

38 He said, "Lord, I believe!" and he worshiped him.

39 Jesus said, "I came into this world for judgment, that those who don't see may see; and that those who see may become blind."

40 Those of the Pharisees who were with him heard these things, and said to him, "Are we also blind?"

41 Jesus said to them, "If you were blind, you would have no sin; but now you say, 'We see.' Therefore your sin remains.

Introduction to Chapter 10

This chapter is one of parables and comparisons. Jesus spoke in parables when He taught. The listener would put himself into the story Jesus shared to learn more about God's ways and His love.

He shared the story of the shepherd and the role of the shepherd. He also shared about the Good Shepherd. The Bible tells us that God is "good". He then shared with us the role of the thief. The thief is the devil. What is the role of the thief?

To steal, kill, and destroy. The thief wants to take away life.

What is the role of The Good Shepherd? The Good Shepherd came to give life.

The Jews could take no more of these comparisons and Jesus putting himself on equal ground with God. He tried to share with them that the works that He did was of God.

It wasn't faith or works.

It wasn't faith and works.

It was faith that works.

They didn't care. They gathered their stones to kill Jesus. Just as they were about to grab Him, Jesus was gone.

John 10:6 Jesus spoke in parables. Parables are not fairy tales. They are stories that relate to actual events that could take place in life, but that the listener can stop and picture him or herself as a character in the story.

John 10:9 The third of Jesus's "I AM..." statements. (See note on John 6:35.) Jesus said "I am the door..." The door allows anyone and everyone to enter and exit. However, each of us must first choose to walk through that door.

CHAPTER 10

"Most certainly, I tell you, one who doesn't enter by the door into the sheep fold, but climbs up some other way, is a thief and a robber. **2** But one who enters in by the door is the shepherd of the sheep. **3** The gatekeeper opens the gate for him, and the sheep listen to his voice. He calls his own sheep by name, and leads them out. **4** Whenever he brings out his own sheep, he goes before them, and the sheep follow him, for they know his voice. **5** They will by no means follow a stranger, but will flee from him; for they don't know the voice of strangers." **6** Jesus spoke this parable to them , but they didn't understand what he was telling them.

7 Jesus therefore said to them again, "Most certainly, I tell you, I am the sheep's door. **8** All who came before me are thieves and robbers, but the sheep didn't listen to them. **9** I am the door. If anyone enters in by me, he will be saved, and will go in and go out, and will find pasture.

10 The thief only comes to steal, kill, and destroy. 😲 I came that they may have life, and may have it abundantly. **11** I am the good shepherd. The good shepherd lays down his life for the sheep. **12** He who is a hired hand, and not a shepherd, who doesn't own the sheep, sees the wolf coming, leaves the sheep, and flees. The wolf snatches the sheep, and scatters them. **13** The hired hand flees because he is a hired hand, and doesn't care for the sheep. **14** I am the good shepherd. 🎛️ I know my own, and I'm known by my own; **15** even as the Father knows me, and I know the Father. I lay down my life for the sheep. **16** I have other sheep, which are not of this fold. I must bring them also, and they will hear my voice. They will become one flock with one shepherd. **17** Therefore the Father loves me, because I lay down my life, that I may take it again. **18** No one takes it away from me, but I lay it down by myself. I have power to lay it down, and I have power to take it

John 10:10 Jesus reminds us that there is also a thief. This is in reference to the devil. What are the devil's intentions? Not to just start us down a bad path, mess with our minds and thoughts, or make us think of evil things. It's way deeper and beyond what we can even imagine. The devil is here to steal, to kill, and to destroy us.

John 10:14 The fourth of Jesus's "I AM..." statements. (See note on John 6:35.) Jesus said "I am the good shepherd.." The shepherd leads and loves every member of the flock.

John 10:19-21
The people are divided on Jesus. Some thought he was crazy. Others pointed to the works that he did, specifically healing. Ask yourself this question: Who is known as the Great Physician? God himself.

John 10:22 The one and only place in the Bible that this feast is know as "The Feast of the Dedication" is in the Gospel of John. Josephus, the Jewish Historian, called it "The Feast of the Lights". This was a feast of joy and the lights were meant to represent that joy, much like we put up lights at Christmas. This feast was in the winter, which, in modern times, would be about the same time we celebrate Christmas today. Today, the Jews would call this "The Feast of Hanukkah".

again. I received this commandment from my Father." **19** Therefore a division arose again among the Jews because of these words. **20** Many of them said, "He has a demon, and is insane! Why do you listen to him?" **21** Others said, "These are not the sayings of one possessed by a demon. It isn't possible for a demon to open the eyes of the blind, is it?"

22 It was the Feast of the Dedication at Jerusalem. **23** It was winter, and Jesus was walking in the temple, in Solomon's porch. **24** The Jews therefore came around him and said to him, "How long will you hold us in suspense? If you are the Christ, tell us plainly."

25 Jesus answered them, "I told you, and you don't believe. The works that I do in my Father's name, these testify about me. **26** But you don't believe, because you are not of my sheep, as I told you. **27** My sheep hear my voice, and I know them, and they follow me.

²⁸ I give eternal life to them. They will never perish, and no one will snatch them out of my hand. ²⁹ My Father who has given them to me is greater than all. No one is able to snatch them out of my Father's hand. ³⁰ I and the Father are one." ³¹ Therefore the Jews took up stones again to stone him. ³² Jesus answered them, "I have shown you many good works from my Father. For which of those works do you stone me?"

³³ The Jews answered him, "We don't stone you for a good work, but for blasphemy: because you, being a man, make yourself God."

³⁴ Jesus answered them, "Isn't it written in your law, 'I said, you are gods?' ³⁵ If he called them gods, to whom the word of God came (and the Scripture can't be broken), ³⁶ do you say of him whom the Father sanctified and sent into the world, 'You blaspheme,' because I said, 'I am the Son of God?' ³⁷ If I don't do the works of my Father, don't believe me.

John 10:29 One of the greatest riddles of all time: Seven letters, Stronger than God, more evil than the devil, rich people want it, poor people have it, if you eat it, you will surely die, what is "it"? This riddle was posed to graduate students that argued for over an hour and still didn't have an answer. They gave the same riddle to a class of first graders and they had the answer in less than a minute. In verse 29, Jesus gives us the answer to the riddle above: nothing. Don't over complicate it! No one, no thing, nothing can pluck you out of the Father's hand! That is how strong our all-powerful God is.

John 10:39 This is the second time that the Jews were going to grab Jesus and kill him. It was also the second time that Jesus left the crowd standing and wondering where He had gone (See notes on John 8:59). Why couldn't they seize Jesus? His hour had not yet come. (See note on John 2:4 and John 7:8)

John 10:42 Despite all the anger toward Jesus, the common man couldn't help but believe. They saw the healings and miracles Jesus performed. They also knew that these signs could only come from God. Because of this, even with what the religious people had stated about Jesus, they believed that Jesus had to be from God.

38 But if I do them, though you don't believe me, believe the works, that you may know and believe that the Father is in me, and I in the Father."

39 They sought again to seize him, and he went out of their hand. **40** He went away again beyond the Jordan into the place where John was baptizing at first, and he stayed there. **41** Many came to him. They said, "John indeed did no sign, but everything that John said about this man is true." **42** Many believed in him there.

The Gospel of John - Chapter 11

If you ever wondered about the human side of Jesus, this is the chapter to read. We see Jesus go through the loss of his friend Lazarus. He experiences the pain and grief of losing a loved one. He also feels the hurt from his friends Mary and Martha who tell Jesus that he wouldn't have died if Jesus had been there.

Jesus does the unheard of and raises Lazarus from the dead. It was, in fact, four days after Lazarus was gone. Because of this, the people in Bethany, where Lazarus lived, believed in Jesus.

This further angered the Pharisees. They didn't want anyone to believe in Jesus, as it threatened their power over the people. Their solution was to seek to kill Jesus.

Jesus knew his time had not yet come. So, because of their plot to kill him, Jesus chose to no longer walk among the Jews until it was His time. Passover was fast approaching. The Pharisees had a sign to seize Jesus upon sight.

Jesus moved out near the wilderness with the disciples. With Passover just around the corner, the Lamb of God was waiting to be the final sacrifice for all.

CHAPTER 11

Now a certain man was sick, Lazarus from Bethany, of the village of Mary and her sister, Martha. **2** It was that Mary who had anointed the Lord with ointment and wiped his feet with her hair, whose brother, Lazarus, was sick. **3** The sisters therefore sent to him, saying, "Lord, behold, he for whom you have great affection is sick." **4** But when Jesus heard it, he said, "This sickness is not to death, but for the glory of God, that God's Son may be glorified by it." **5** Now Jesus loved Martha, and her sister, and Lazarus.

6 When therefore he heard that he was sick, he stayed two days in the place where he was. **7** Then after this he said to the disciples, "Let's go into Judea again."

8 The disciples asked him, "Rabbi, the Jews were just trying to stone you. Are you going there again?"

9 Jesus answered, "Aren't there twelve hours of daylight? If a man walks in the day, he

John 11:2 This is one of the most controversial and talked about events to take place in the New Testament, both then and now! (See note on John 12:3 and John 12:2-6) Jesus raised four people from the dead: the widow's son (Luke 7:35), the synagogue ruler's daughter (Mark 5:42), Himself, and Lazarus. Why is this one significant? Because of how long Lazarus had been dead, which was four days. (See note on John 11:39)

John 11:5 we have to remember that Jesus was both God and man. Often times we forget the part of him being a person just like you and me. This verse shows not only the love that Jesus had for this family, but that Jesus had people that he cared for deeply outside of the 12 disciples.

doesn't stumble, because he sees the light of this world. **10** But if a man walks in the night, he stumbles, because the light isn't in him." **11** He said these things, and after that, he said to them, "Our friend, Lazarus, has fallen asleep, but I am going so that I may awake him out of sleep."

12 The disciples therefore said, "Lord, if he has fallen asleep, he will recover."
13 Now Jesus had spoken of his death, but they thought that he spoke of taking rest in sleep. **14** So Jesus said to them plainly then, "Lazarus is dead.

15 I am glad for your sakes that I was not there, so that you may believe. Nevertheless, let's go to him." **16** Thomas therefore, who is called Didymus, said to his fellow disciples,
"Let's go also, that we may die with him."

17 So when Jesus came, he found that he had been in the tomb four days already. **18** Now Bethany was near Jerusalem, about fifteen

84

John 11:14 Even though Jesus and his disciples spoke the same language, there were many times that Jesus had to explain things further for them to understand. Here, Lazarus was sick and they thought he was asleep and would wake up after lying down for a nap. Jesus explained to them the sleep they discussed was actually death. Now that the disciples understood this, they realized they were going to a funeral. As we will see in the next chapter, however, a funeral was not what took place.

John 11:16 In typical Thomas fashion, he made a statement that others criticized him for being one of doubt. The flipside is that he was also one of courage. We are not sure who he was referring to here that the disciples would go and die with in going to see Lazarus. It could be Jesus as they had tried to stone him previously. And it could have been Lazarus who was already dead. Either way, Thomas had encouraged the disciples that they all join Jesus on this trip. Thomas also prepared them for what could be the worst outcome.

John 11:21 Here we get to see a woman that believed in the power God had given his son Jesus. Even though she was not one of the 12 disciples, Martha had heard and seen enough of the signs that Jesus had performed that she knew in her heart (had faith) that had Jesus been there her brother would still be alive.

John 11:25 This is the fifth of seven "I AM..." statements that Jesus defined. (See original note on John 6:35)

stadia away. **19** Many of the Jews had joined the women around Martha and Mary, to console them concerning their brother. **20** Then when Martha heard that Jesus was coming, she went and met him, but Mary stayed in the house. **21** Therefore Martha said to Jesus, "Lord, if you would have been here, my brother wouldn't have died.

22 Even now I know that whatever you ask of God, God will give you." **23** Jesus said to her, "Your brother will rise again."

24 Martha said to him, "I know that he will rise again in the resurrection at the last day."

25 Jesus said to her, "I am the resurrection and the life. He who believes in me will still live, even if he dies. **26** Whoever lives and believes in me will never die. Do you believe this?"

27 She said to him, "Yes, Lord. I have come to believe that you are the Christ, God's Son, he who comes into the world."

28 When she had said this, she went away and called Mary, her sister, secretly, saying, "The Teacher is here and is calling you." **29** When she heard this, she arose quickly, and went to him. **30** Now Jesus had not yet come into the village, but was in the place where Martha met him. **31** Then the Jews who were with her in the house, and were consoling her, when they saw Mary, that she rose up quickly and went out, followed her, saying, "She is going to the tomb to weep there."

32 Therefore when Mary came to where Jesus was and saw him,
she fell down at his feet, saying to him, "Lord, if you would have been here, my brother wouldn't have died."

John 11:27 Here was an example of the depth of Martha's faith. She understood that Jesus was the resurrection in both the here and now and forever. She also professed that Jesus was not only the one that all of Israel had been looking for to save them, but that Jesus was also God's son that was sent down to the very world in which we live.

John 11:31 Notice who was consoling Mary at this time? The Jews. It doesn't say her friends and family. Why? It could have been because at this time and in this culture, mourners were hired by family members to attend funeral services, which could be weeklong events.

John 11:35 This is the shortest verse in the Bible. Yet with just two words, it captures the emotions of Jesus. Here we once again get to see the human side of Jesus (See note on John 4:6-8). The shortest verse of the Bible shares the love and compassion that Jesus had for people. When you read on in verse 36, even the Jews noticed the love and compassion Jesus had. The hatred for him continued as they mocked Jesus with their words, at a time when Jesus was obviously grieving.

John 11:39 A body would decompose and the smell of the rotting flesh would have already taken place. The Jews believed that this would happen starting three days after a death. This being the fourth day, it would have surely occurred by this time.

33 When Jesus therefore saw her weeping, and the Jews weeping who came with her, he groaned in the spirit, and was troubled, **34** and said, "Where have you laid him?"

They told him, "Lord, come and see."

35 Jesus wept.

36 The Jews therefore said, "See how much affection he had for him!" **37** Some of them said, "Couldn't this man, who opened the eyes of him who was blind, have also kept this man from dying?"

38 Jesus therefore, again groaning in himself, came to the tomb. Now it was a cave, and a stone lay against it. **39** Jesus said, "Take away the stone."

Martha, the sister of him who was dead, said to him, "Lord, by this time there is a stench, for he has been dead four days."

40 Jesus said to her, "Didn't I tell you that if you believed, you would see God's glory?"

41 So they took away the stone from the place where the dead man was lying. Jesus lifted up his eyes, and said, "Father, I thank you that you listened to me.

42 I know that you always listen to me, but because of the multitude standing around I said this, that they may believe that you sent me." **43** When he had said this, he cried with a loud voice, "Lazarus, come out!"

44 He who was dead came out, bound hand and foot with wrappings, and his face was wrapped around with a cloth.

Jesus said to them, "Free him, and let him go."

45 Therefore many of the Jews who came to Mary and saw what Jesus did believed in him.

46 But some of them went away to the Pharisees and told them the things which Jesus had done. **47** The chief priests therefore and the Pharisees gathered a council, and said, "What are we doing? For this man does many signs. **48** If we leave him alone like this, everyone will believe in him, and

John 11:41 Jesus refers to God as his "Father" over 100 times in the Gospel of John alone. This is one instance that Jesus actually speaks publicly to his Father.

John 11:44 The wrappings that Lazarus wore were his burial clothes. These are the same kind of clothes that Jesus will wear when he is buried.

John 11:45 This is the last of Jesus's recorded miracles/signs in the Gospel of John that was performed before his death. (See note for all seven miracles, or signs, in John 2:11) His biggest miracle, in the eyes of many, was his last one. It would be a sign of signs, as it signaled what would also take place after Jesus's death.

John 11:49-53 In the end, who put Jesus to death? The high priest and his disciples did. The most religious of the religious and his religious followers put one man to death for us all. (See note on John 3:16)

John 11:55 Passover is still a very important Festival in Jerusalem to this day. There are seven that are celebrated each year, with Passover being the most attended (See note on John 7:2 for more on the festivals.) The story of Passover can be found in Exodus 12, which tells us that the Angel of the Lord passed over the houses of everyone in Egypt, and whoever had the blood of the lamb on the doorpost would be saved. Jesus, the Son of God, the Lamb of God, would soon shed his blood so that all that believe would not perish but live forever (See note on John 3:16).

the Romans will come and take away both our place and our nation."

49 But a certain one of them, Caiaphas, being high priest that year, said to them, "You know nothing at all, **50** nor do you consider that it is advantageous for us that one man should die for the people, and that the whole nation not perish." **51** Now he didn't say this of himself, but being high priest that year, he prophesied that Jesus would die for the nation, **52** and not for the nation only, but that he might also gather together into one the children of God who are scattered abroad. **53** So from that day forward they took counsel that they might put him to death.

54 Jesus therefore walked no more openly among the Jews, but departed from there into the country near the wilderness, to a city called Ephraim. He stayed there with his disciples. **55** Now the Passover of the Jews was at hand. Many went up from the country to Jerusalem before the Passover, to purify themselves.

56 Then they sought for Jesus and spoke with one another as they stood in the temple, "What do you think—that he isn't coming to the feast at all?" **57** Now the chief priests and the Pharisees had commanded that if anyone knew where he was, he should report it, that they might seize him.

John 11:55-57 Look at what takes place in these verses. The Pharisees are going to the feast to purify, meaning clean, themselves before God. But they are also going to prepare to capture Jesus. There will be an estimated 2.5 million people at Passover. There will be an estimated 250,000 lambs slaughtered at this time. In the midst of it all will be one man, the Lamb of God, who was willing to come and die and be the sacrifice for each of them – and for the whole world.

Introduction to Chapter 12

The tension is mounting. One of the twelve, Judas, is starting to question events that are surrounding Jesus and the disciples. It isn't about what took place, rather, the money that could have been made.

Jesus rides into Jerusalem on a donkey. It is what many call his triumphal entry. The crowds cheer for him and wave and lay palm branches on the ground before him. It is an entry fit only for a king.

Because of this, the Pharisees fear that Jesus is about to set up a political kingdom in Jerusalem. They do everything they can to oppose him. They even plot to kill Lazarus, as him being raised from the dead caused more people to believe in Jesus.

So, what does Jesus do with all of the fanfare, publicity, and king's welcome? He predicts that He will die soon. Suddenly, Jesus and the people around him hear a voice. They believe it is an angel.

Who is it that spoke at this time so that all could hear? Who is it that would show up at such a time as this?

It was God Himself, speaking from Heaven above who came to his Son when His hour had finally come. In the moment Jesus needed to hear from his Father the most, His Heavenly Father was there.

John 12:3 There was a lot happening all at one time as pictured in this verse. Mary took the most expensive item she had and used the most honored part of her body (her hair), to apply the ointment to the lowest and dirtiest part of Jesus's body (his feet). She understood the sacrifice Jesus was about to make, and in turn, made the greatest sacrifice she could make to him.

John 12:2-6 Just as we saw in John 11:48 (see note), people were starting to focus on their own power and prestige and what was in it for them. Judas, one of the twelve, one of those closest to Jesus, and their treasurer, wasn't focused on the poor and needy. He was focused on the money and himself. We will soon see just how far he was willing to go for the money that was missing from the treasury at this point.

CHAPTER 12

Then six days before the Passover, Jesus came to Bethany, where Lazarus was, who had been dead, whom he raised from the dead. **2** So they made him a supper there. Martha served, but Lazarus was one of those who sat at the table with him. **3** Therefore Mary took a pound of ointment of pure nard, very precious, and anointed Jesus's feet and wiped his feet with her hair. The house was filled with the fragrance of the ointment. **4** Then Judas Iscariot, Simon's son, one of his disciples, who would betray him, said, **5** "Why wasn't this ointment sold for three hundred denarii, and given to the poor?" **6** Now he said this, not because he cared for the poor, but because he was a thief, and having the money box, used to steal what was put into it. **7** But Jesus said, "Leave her alone. She has kept this for the day of my burial.

8 For you always have the poor with you, but you don't always have me."

9 A large crowd therefore of the Jews learned that he was there, and they came, not for Jesus' sake only, but that they might see Lazarus also, whom he had raised from the dead. **10** But the chief priests conspired to put Lazarus to death also, **11** because on account of him many of the Jews went away and believed in Jesus. **12** On the next day a great multitude had come to the feast. When they heard that Jesus was coming to Jerusalem, **13** they took the branches of the palm trees and went out to meet him, and cried out, "Hosanna! Blessed is he who comes in the name of the Lord, the King of Israel!"

14 Jesus, having found a young donkey, sat on it. As it is written, **15** "Don't be afraid, daughter of Zion. Behold, your King comes, sitting on a donkey's colt." **16** His disciples didn't understand these things at first, but when Jesus was glorified, then they

John 12:13 The words that the Jews were crying out were from Psalm 118: 25-26 "Save us now, we beg you Yahweh!" The words in Hebrew were pronounced "Hosanna".

John 12:15 Ecclesiastes 3 tells us there is a time for everything under the sun. Jesus picked this time to come into Jerusalem in such a way that it could only point to one thing: the Messiah the Jews had been looking for and waiting on for many generations was here. He even proclaimed who He was at this time, so there wouldn't be any doubt. Somehow, all of the people there, including Jesus's disciples, didn't understand and still missed it.

John 12:16 In this verse we get a picture of the writer John being a disciple of Jesus, yet not completely grasping that role. In the words John uses, we can both sense and hear the emotion from John not truly understanding Jesus while He was still alive. Like many others, it took both Jesus's death and resurrection for them to truly embrace Him not only as their friend, but also as their Lord and Savior.

John 12:23 This is the transition verse as Jesus let's the disciples know that the visitations, the meetings, the miracles, etc., are over. Up to this point, Jesus shared that his hour had not yet come (See note on John 2:4). For the first time, he has let those closest to Him know that his hour had arrived.

remembered that these things were written about him, and that they had done these things to him. **17** The multitude therefore that was with him when he called Lazarus out of the tomb and raised him from the dead was testifying about it. **18** For this cause also the multitude went and met him, because they heard that he had done this sign. **19** The Pharisees therefore said among themselves, "See how you accomplish nothing. Behold, the world has gone after him."

20 Now there were certain Greeks among those who went up to worship at the feast. **21** These, therefore, came to Philip, who was from Bethsaida of Galilee, and asked him, saying, "Sir, we want to see Jesus." **22** Philip came and told Andrew, and in turn, Andrew came with Philip, and they told Jesus. **23** Jesus answered them, "The time has come for the Son of Man to be glorified.

24 Most certainly I tell you, unless a grain of wheat falls into the earth and dies, it remains by itself alone. But if it dies, it bears much fruit. **25** He who loves his life will lose it. He who hates his life in this world will keep it to eternal life. **26** If anyone serves me, let him follow me. Where I am, there my servant will also be. If anyone serves me, the Father will honor him.

27 "Now my soul is troubled. What shall I say? 'Father, save me from this time?' But I came to this time for this cause. **28** Father, glorify your name!" Then a voice came out of the sky, saying, "I have both glorified it, and will glorify it again."

29 Therefore the multitude who stood by and heard it said that it had thundered. Others said, "An angel has spoken to him."

30 Jesus answered, "This voice hasn't come for my sake, but for your sakes. **31** Now is the judgment of this world. Now the prince of this world will be cast

John 12:27 When people talk about Christianity, their issues aren't with Jesus. They love the human side of Jesus that we read about in the Bible. He is kind, compassionate, and lives with empathy. Jesus knows he will soon be walking to His death, and that He will be doing so for all of us. In his soul, Jesus is troubled, just as each of us, regardless of race, gender, or religious affiliation would be if we were walking in his shoes.

John 12:28 When Jesus was baptized, a voice from Heaven spoke. The voice didn't say "I am God.." The voice just spoke. Here Jesus speaks to His Father, and His father replies.

John 12:29 This shows us that the same frustrations took place at this time as they do now. In verse 28 God shows up in a mighty way. By verse 29, the people are already pointing to something other than God. Some point to nature, such as thunder, while others point to things that are of God, such as angels. In the end, both would be because of God, yet He rarely gets the credit He has both earned and deserves.

John 12:34 The word "Christ", meaning the anointed one, shows up over 500 times in the New Testament. You find the name "Jesus", meaning savior, over 900 times in the New Testament.

John 12:38-39 Isaiah was a prophet from the Old Testament. You can read the book that bears his name in the Bible. The people surrounding Jesus had been looking for the Christ. Generation after generation had come and gone waiting for the one that would deliver them. Now that he was finally here before them, even after hearing God's voice (see note on John 12:28) and witnessing his miracles, they didn't believe.

out. **32** And I, if I am lifted up from the earth, will draw all people to myself." **33** But he said this, signifying by what kind of death he should die. **34** The multitude answered him, "We have heard out of the law that the Christ remains forever. How do you say, 'The Son of Man must be lifted up?' Who is this Son of Man?"

35 Jesus therefore said to them, "Yet a little while the light is with you. Walk while you have the light, that darkness doesn't overtake you. He who walks in the darkness doesn't know where he is going. **36** While you have the light, believe in the light, that you may become children of light." Jesus said these things, and he departed and hid himself from them. **37** But though he had done so many signs before them, yet they didn't believe in him, **38** that the word of Isaiah the prophet might be fulfilled, which he spoke, "Lord, who has believed our report?

To whom has the arm of the Lord been revealed?"

³⁹ For this cause they couldn't believe, for Isaiah said again,
⁴⁰ "He has blinded their eyes and he hardened their heart,
lest they should see with their eyes, and perceive with their heart, and would turn,
and I would heal them."

⁴¹ Isaiah said these things when he saw his glory, and spoke of him. ⁴² Nevertheless even many of the rulers believed in him, but because of the Pharisees they didn't confess it, so that they wouldn't be put out of the synagogue, ⁴³ for they loved men's praise more than God's praise.

⁴⁴ Jesus cried out and said, "Whoever believes in me, believes not in me, but in him who sent me. ⁴⁵ He who sees me sees him who sent me. ⁴⁶ I have come as a light into the world, that whoever believes in me may not remain in the darkness. ⁴⁷ If anyone listens to my sayings, and doesn't believe, I don't judge him.

John 12:40 You can read these words about Jesus in Isaiah 6:10. They were written over 700 years before Jesus was born.

John 12:43 The very central verse of the Bible is Psalm 118:8. It is a reminder of the very issue that is still prevalent today: it is better to take refuge in God than to put your trust in man.

John 12:43 A great question to ask yourself daily is "Who am I trying to please?" A great follow up to that question is this: Would you rather be a "people pleaser" or a "God pleaser"?

For I came not to judge the world, but to save the world.

👍 **48** He who rejects me, and doesn't receive my sayings, has one who judges him. The word that I spoke will judge him in the last day. **49** For I spoke not from myself, but the Father who sent me, he gave me a commandment, what I should say, and what I should speak. **50** I know that his commandment is eternal life. The things therefore which I speak, even as the Father has said to me, so I speak."

Introduction to Chapter 13

It is the night before the death of Jesus. According to the book of Luke, chapter 22, Jesus eagerly awaited this time. He looked forward to one last dinner with His friends, even though He knew what was coming next.

Jesus does the unthinkable and fills a basin full of water. He will wash his disciples' feet, even though they try to stop Him. It is the ultimate act of being a servant, especially for the one that was just honored as a king riding into Jerusalem.

After washing their feet, Jesus identifies two of His disciples for the worst acts ever done to Jesus outside of his crucifixion. Jesus identifies Judas as the one that would betray Him. Jesus also tells Peter that he will deny Him three times the next day.

Between identifying the two for the sins they are about to commit, Jesus gives the disciples a New Commandment. There is no "Thou Shalt Not..." (Exodus 20 or Deuteronomy 5 gives a the list of the Ten Commandments) in the new commandment Jesus shares with them. They are to love one another. It comes with a second part to the commandment, and that is that they are to love one another as Jesus loved each of them, despite their betrayal and denials.

John 13:1 In this verse, we see the emotions of the writer, John. Remember, this letter was not written until many years after the death and resurrection of Jesus. Looking back, John writes to each one of us that Jesus knew what was coming, yet, as we will see later in this Gospel, he loved them to the very end.

John 13:2 Never forget that God allowed the devil to rule this world. By sending Jesus into this same world, He gives each of us the opportunity to choose. It isn't high level math or quantum physics. It is simply a choice. In this verse we see the choice Judas made. One of the 12 disciples chose the prince of this world, the devil, over the King of Eternity, God.

CHAPTER 13

Now before the feast of the Passover, Jesus, knowing that his time had come that he would depart from this world to the Father, having loved his own who were in the world, he loved them to the end. ² During supper, the devil having already put into the heart of Judas Iscariot, Simon's son, to betray him, ³ Jesus, knowing that the Father had given all things into his hands, and that he came from God, and was going to God, ⁴ arose from supper, and laid aside his outer garments. He took a towel and wrapped a towel around his waist. ⁵ Then he poured water into the basin, and began to wash the disciples' feet and to wipe them with the towel that was wrapped around him. ⁶ Then he came to Simon Peter. He said to him, "Lord, do you wash my feet?"

⁷ Jesus answered him, "You don't know what I am doing now, but you will understand later."

8 Peter said to him, "You will never wash my feet!"

Jesus answered him, "If I don't wash you, you have no part with me."

9 Simon Peter said to him, "Lord, not my feet only, but also my hands and my head!"

10 Jesus said to him, "Someone who has bathed only needs to have his feet washed, but is completely clean. You are clean, but not all of you." **11** For he knew him who would betray him, therefore he said, "You are not all clean." **12** So when he had washed their feet, put his outer garment back on, and sat down again, he said to them, "Do you know what I have done to you? **13** You call me, 'Teacher' and 'Lord.' You say so correctly, for so I am. **14** If I then, the Lord and the Teacher, have washed your feet, you also ought to wash one another's feet. **15** For I have given you an example, that you should also do as I have done to you. **16** Most certainly I tell you,

John 13:3-8 Here is a part of communion that we often forget and take for granted. Jesus stopped and showed the disciples that He was their servant leader. He led by example, and took the role of the servant and, even through them trying to stop Him, stooped down and washed each of their feet. All the sand, dirt, and any other thing that they may have stepped in along the way to the supper, Jesus made clean.

John 13:11 Jesus washed all of the disciples' feet. He didn't pick and choose the ones he wanted to make clean. That means he washed Judas's feet, the one that would betray him, before sending him off to turn his back on God.

👍 John 13:12-17 First we see in verse 12 that Jesus sat down. When the Teacher sits, it means it is time for a lesson. He reveals to his disciples the lesson in verse 17: it isn't enough to know the teachings of Jesus. The disciples then and the disciples now need to "do them" and put them into practice in their every day lives.

😔 John 13:23 The disciple Jesus loved is the author of the book you are reading: John. After this teaching moment, rather than sit back and talk, John showed his choice by doing. He chose to turn into and place his head on the one that not only loved him, but that John loved, as well. When you aren't sure of what choice to make in life, turning your head and resting in Jesus is always the right choice to make. Always.

a servant is not greater than his lord, neither is one who is sent greater than he who sent him. **17** If you know these things, blessed are you if you do them.

👍 **18** I don't speak concerning all of you. I know whom I have chosen. But that the Scripture may be fulfilled, 'He who eats bread with me has lifted up his heel against me.' **19** From now on, I tell you before it happens, that when it happens, you may believe that I am he. **20** Most certainly I tell you, he who receives whomever I send, receives me; and he who receives me, receives him who sent me."

21 When Jesus had said this, he was troubled in spirit, and testified, "Most certainly I tell you that one of you will betray me."

22 The disciples looked at one another, perplexed about whom he spoke. **23** One of his disciples, whom Jesus loved, was at the table, leaning against Jesus' breast. 😔

24 Simon Peter therefore beckoned to him, and said to him, "Tell us who it is of whom he speaks." **25** He, leaning back, as he was, on Jesus' breast, asked him, "Lord, who is it?"

26 Jesus therefore answered, "It is he to whom I will give this piece of bread when I have dipped it." So when he had dipped the piece of bread, he gave it to Judas, the son of Simon Iscariot. 👍 **27** After the piece of bread, then Satan entered into him. Then Jesus said to him, "What you do, do quickly."

28 Now nobody at the table knew why he said this to him. **29** For some thought, because Judas had the money box, that Jesus said to him, "Buy what things we need for the feast," or that he should give something to the poor. 😮

30 Therefore having received that morsel, he went out immediately. It was night. 😒 **31** When he had gone out, Jesus said, "Now the Son of Man has been glorified, and God has been glorified in him.

👍 John 13:26 This verse can be a source of argument between believers and non-believers. In Matthew 26:13, it stated that the one who betrayed Jesus was the one that dipped his bread at the same time as Jesus. In John, the writer stated that it was Jesus that dipped the bread and handed it to Judas. Which was correct? Both were. The verses were from the perspective of the authors. How do we know that both were correct? In every gospel and in every teaching in and outside of the Bible, it was Judas that ended up being the betrayer.

😮 John 13:29 In Matthew 6:24, Jesus said we cannot serve both God and money. Here we see the role Judas had within the 12 disciples. He handled the money. By choosing to betray Jesus, he showed were his loyalty was.

😒 John 13:30 John noted that when Judas made his move, he did so at night. This doesn't mean, as has been taught by many cultures, that nothing good comes at night. It just meant that when Judas chose to betray Jesus, he did so at the time when the light wouldn't be present.

👍 John 13:34 The commandments the people were used to hearing were the things they shouldn't do, such as "Thou shalt not kill." (A list of the Ten Commandments can be found in Exodus 20:1-17 and Deuteronomy 5:4-21) Jesus gives them a commandment they should do: love one another. For an example of what it means to love, Jesus uses Himself as the example. The commandment for each of us is to love others as Jesus loved others.

#️⃣ John 13:37-38 Peter goes from stating he would lay his life down for Jesus to Jesus letting Peter know that he would deny Him not once, not twice, but three times before the sun would rise the next day.

32 If God has been glorified in him, God will also glorify him in himself, and he will glorify him immediately. **33** Little children, I will be with you a little while longer. You will seek me, and as I said to the Jews, 'Where I am going, you can't come,' so now I tell you. **34** 👍 A new commandment I give to you, that you love one another. Just as I have loved you, you also love one another. **35** By this everyone will know that you are my disciples, if you have love for one another."

36 Simon Peter said to him, "Lord, where are you going?"

Jesus answered, "Where I am going, you can't follow now, but you will follow afterwards."

37 Peter said to him, "Lord, why can't I follow you now? I will lay down my life for you."

38 Jesus answered him, "Will you lay down your life for me? Most certainly I tell you, the rooster won't crow until you have denied me three times. #️⃣

Introduction to Chapter 14

Throughout the entire Gospel, Jesus has talked about his relationship with God, his Heavenly Father. The disciples are at the point where Jesus leaving them is about to become a reality. They have been discipled by Jesus to this point, and his leaving means they will have to face the same people that hated Jesus moving forward on their own.

Jesus realizes they have fears and uses this as a time to teach them that even though He is going to leave them physically, He will still be with them. But, He also has a place He has to go and is preparing a place for them, as well.

It is at this time that Jesus brings the third part of the Trinity to the disciples. Jesus shares with them that when He leaves that God will send the Holy Spirit in His place. The Holy Spirit will be there to counsel and comfort the disciples.

Even though the disciples have learned so much in their time of ministry with Jesus, it is necessary for Him to leave so that they might receive His Spirit. In exchange for the death of Jesus, the disciples will be left with not only the Holy Spirit, but with the peace that only Jesus could promise.

John 14:1 Jesus would soon be walking to his death. Yet He chooses to stop and teach His disciples. In difficult times, remember the instructions He gives here: instead of being troubled in your heart, believe God has control of the situation, and remember the example Jesus led when his heart would have been troubled.

John 14:5 Many times Thomas gets a bad rap. He is the reason we have the term "Doubting Thomas". Yet, in this time of trouble, he was the one of the twelve that spoke up to ask the question we would all want to ask in this situation. There are times like this one when we should look at the courage of Thomas, too!

John 14:6 This is the sixth of seven "I AM..." statements that Jesus defined. (See original note on John 6:35.)

CHAPTER 14

"Don't let your heart be troubled. Believe in God. Believe also in me. ² In my Father's house are many homes. If it weren't so, I would have told you. I am going to prepare a place for you. ³ If I go and prepare a place for you, I will come again, and will receive you to myself; that where I am, you may be there also. ⁴ You know where I go, and you know the way."

⁵ Thomas said to him, "Lord, we don't know where you are going. How can we know the way?"

⁶ Jesus said to him, "I am the way, the truth, and the life. No one comes to the Father, except through me. ⁷ If you had known me, you would have known my Father also. From now on, you know him, and have seen him."

⁸ Philip said to him, "Lord, show us the Father, and that will be enough for us."

⁹ Jesus said to him, "Have I been with you such a long time, and do you not know me, Philip?

He who has seen me has seen the Father. How do you say, 'Show us the Father?' **10** Don't you believe that I am in the Father, and the Father in me? The words that I tell you, I speak not from myself; but the Father who lives in me does his works. **11** Believe me that I am in the Father, and the Father in me; or else believe me for the very works' sake.

12 Most certainly I tell you, he who believes in me, the works that I do, he will do also; and he will do greater works than these, because I am going to my Father. **13** Whatever you will ask in my name, I will do it, that the Father may be glorified in the Son. **14** If you will ask anything in my name, I will do it. **15** If you love me, keep my commandments. **16** I will pray to the Father, and he will give you another Counselor, that he may be with you forever: **17** the Spirit of truth, whom the world can't receive; for it doesn't see him and doesn't know him. You know him, for he lives with you, and will be in you. **18** I will not

John 14:9-11 One of the most difficult parts of Christianity to understand is the Trinity: God the Father, Jesus the Son, and the Holy Spirit. How can the three exist as one? The words of Jesus here share that they exist through one another. Many see the mathematical equation as $1+1+1=1$, and it doesn't add up to them, as we all know $1+1+1=3$. If this is confusing to you, remember that they exist because of one another, so the equation is actually $1x1x1=1$.

John 14:16 The man Jesus could minister to people one-on-one or to a small group or even a large crowd, such as when he fed 5,000 men and their wives and children. Jesus shared with those listening that when he died physically, that God would send the Holy Spirit to minister in His place. The Holy Spirit can minister to any number of people at any time, and can teach us, counsel us, and show us God's truth, and will be with believers forever.

John 14:22 Judas (not Iscariot)? There is more than one Judas in the Bible? Just as there is more than one John, more than one Mary, yes there is more than one Judas. People today wouldn't name their son Judas because of the Judas that betrayed Jesus in the Bible. But, yes, there was a Judas that was also a disciple that was good. Sadly, he was not the Judas that we remember to this day.

John 14:22 By the words used here, we can see that this is not Judas Iscariot. He had already left the other disciples (see John 13:30). This Judas could be Thaddeus, another disciple known as Judas Thaddeus, or Jude, the brother of James and half brother of Jesus, who wrote the book of Jude. It is possible that Jude and Judas Thaddeus are the same person, although we do not know for certain.

leave you orphans. I will come to you. **19** Yet a little while, and the world will see me no more; but you will see me. Because I live, you will live also. **20** In that day you will know that I am in my Father, and you in me, and I in you. **21** One who has my commandments and keeps them, that person is one who loves me. One who loves me will be loved by my Father, and I will love him, and will reveal myself to him."

22 Judas (not Iscariot) said to him, "Lord, what has happened that you are about to reveal yourself to us, and not to the world?"

23 Jesus answered him, "If a man loves me, he will keep my word. My Father will love him, and we will come to him, and make our home with him. **24** He who doesn't love me doesn't keep my words. The word which you hear isn't mine, but the Father's who sent me. **25** I have said these things to you while still living with you. **26** But the Counselor, the Holy Spirit, whom the Father will send in my name, will teach you all things, and will remind you of all that I said to you. **27** Peace I leave with you. My peace I give to you; not as the world gives, I give to you. Don't let your heart be troubled, neither let it be fearful. **28** You heard how I told you, 'I go away, and I come to you.' If you loved me, you would have rejoiced, because I said 'I am going to my Father;' for the Father is greater than I. **29** Now I have told you before it happens so that when it happens, you may believe. **30** I will no more speak much with you, for the prince of the world comes, and he has nothing in me. **31** But that the world may know that I love the Father, and as the Father commanded me, even so I do. Arise, let's go from here.

John 14:27 Other versions of the Bible interpret "neither let it be fearful" as "do not be afraid". The term "do not be afraid" shows up 365 times in the Bible. It is a daily reminder that through the counsel of the Holy Spirit that Jesus promised and God sent us (read verse 14:26), that in our heart we can rest in the peace that God brings us and there is no need to be afraid or fearful!

John 14:31 Jesus has been sitting with his disciples to this point. He starts the last sentence of this chapter with "Arise, let's go..." It is at this point that Jesus starts to walk toward His death, and he knows it. From this point on, knowing he has been sentenced to death, he is literally a "dead man walking".

Introduction to Chapter 15

In the Old Testament, Israel was referred to as the vine. The Jews felt they were connected to God because they belonged to Israel. But Israel didn't produce the fruit that God wanted them to produce.

Jesus, however, was different. He explained to the Jews that He was the true vine, and that God was actually the vinedresser. As believers, we are to produce good fruit. That means Godly fruit. One of two things will happen to the branches, which believers are. They will either bear fruit and be pruned by God to bear more fruit, or the branch will be cut off and...well, you have to read on to see what happens to those branches.

The point to remember about the vine and its branches is this: apart from the vine, the branches can do nothing on their own. The branches need the vine for nourishment and growth.

As a believer, we are called for more than just praying and studying. We are to grow in our walk with God and to help others grow in their walk with God. He expected this from His disciples then, and it is expected of His disciples now.

John 15:1 This is the final "I AM..." statement that Jesus defined. (See original note on John 6:35) To summarize, Jesus says in the book of John "I am...": the bread of life (John 6:35, 48, 51); the light of the world (John 8:12, 9:5); the door (John 10:7, 9), the good shepherd (John 10:11, 14); the resurrection and the life (John 11:25); the way, the truth, and the life (John 14:6); and, finally, the true vine (John 15:1).

John 15:8 How do you know if you are a true disciple? Jesus explains it here in this verse: you will bear fruit that will reflect God. Remember, you may be the only way a person sees God at times, so take the time to cultivate those relationships and see God's fruit grow through you!

CHAPTER 15

"I am the true vine, and my Father is the farmer. 2 Every branch in me that doesn't bear fruit, he takes away. Every branch that bears fruit, he prunes, that it may bear more fruit. 3 You are already pruned clean because of the word which I have spoken to you. 4 Remain in me, and I in you. As the branch can't bear fruit by itself unless it remains in the vine, so neither can you, unless you remain in me. 5 I am the vine. You are the branches. He who remains in me and I in him bears much fruit, for apart from me you can do nothing. 6 If a man doesn't remain in me, he is thrown out as a branch and is withered; and they gather them, throw them into the fire, and they are burned. 7 If you remain in me, and my words remain in you, you will ask whatever you desire, and it will be done for you.

8 "In this my Father is glorified, that you bear much fruit; and so you will be my disciples.
9 Even as the Father

has loved me, I also have loved you. Remain in my love. **10** If you keep my commandments, you will remain in my love; even as I have kept my Father's commandments, and remain in his love. **11** I have spoken these things to you, that my joy may remain in you, and that your joy may be made full. **12** "This is my commandment, that you love one another, even as I have loved you. **13** Greater love has no one than this, that someone lay down his life for his friends.

14 You are my friends, if you do whatever I command everything that I heard from my Father, I have made known to you. you. **15** No longer do I call you servants, for the servant doesn't know what his lord does. But I have called you friends, for **16** You didn't choose me, but I chose you and appointed you, that you should go and bear fruit, and that your fruit should remain; that whatever you will ask of the Father in my name, he may give it to you.

John 15:11 If you have ever been to Sunday school, you have probably heard the easiest way to remember what JOY is: Jesus. Others. You. Let's expand on that a little: Love Jesus, Serve Others, Rest in and embrace the joy that the first two bring to You!

John 15:12 When you want to know the example of *how* to love others, all you have to do is use the example of how Jesus loved others! Any time at any place with anyone. Jesus always looked for the opportunity, whether it was the hottest part of the day or in the cool of the evening, there was always an opportunity to show God's love to someone.

John 15:13 Love: Verse 11 gives us the easy to remember model, verse 12 gives us the example of how, and verse 13 gives us the example of what. What does love look like? Sacrifice. It could be small, it could be big, but putting down what is important for you to give whatever you can to help someone who is in need.

John 15:18 One of the themes of the lesson Jesus shares here is hate. Hate is the opposite of love. To show hatred means there is action behind it. The hatred that is discussed here was not only the feeling in one's heart, but the pursuit of showing that hatred by taking it out on others.

John 15:17-25 In this passage the word hate is repeated eight times. If 1 Corinthians 13 is the love chapter, this section of John would be the hate passage. In this world, you can't have good without bad or bad without good. Sadly, even though Jesus loved everyone and showed it with his kindness, compassion, and teachings, many hated him in return.

17 "I command these things to you, that you may love one another. **18** If the world hates you, you know that it has hated me before it hated you. **19** If you were of the world, the world would love its own. But because you are not of the world, since I chose you out of the world, therefore the world hates you. **20** Remember the word that I said to you: 'A servant is not greater than his lord.' If they persecuted me, they will also persecute you. If they kept my word, they will also keep yours. **21** But they will do all these things to you for my name's sake, because they don't know him who sent me. **22** If I had not come and spoken to them, they would not have had sin; but now they have no excuse for their sin. **23** He who hates me, hates my Father also. **24** If I hadn't done among them the works which no one else did, they wouldn't have had sin. But now they have seen and also hated both me and my Father. **25** But this happened so that the word may be fulfilled which was written in their law, 'They hated me without a cause.'

26 "When the Counselor 👍 has come, whom I will send to you from the Father, the Spirit of truth, who proceeds from the Father, he will testify about me. 27 You will also testify, because you have been with me from the beginning. 😦

👍 John 15:26 Notice that "Counselor", "Spirit", and "Father are all capitalized. They refer to a person. That person is God himself. God is there for each of us to give us His Counsel (or Comfort), His Spirit, and to be our Heavenly Father!

😦 John 15:26-27 The word testify doesn't mean what we see in the movies or on TV in a court case. In the Bible, it refers to something happening that only God could make happen. When that happened, people couldn't help but testify, or give credit to God and God alone for making it happen.

Introduction to Chapter 16

Jesus is spending His final moments with those he was closest to. We know them as the twelve disciples. But, remember, to Jesus, they were also His best friends.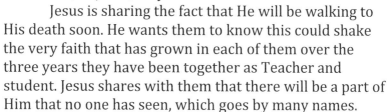

Jesus is sharing the fact that He will be walking to His death soon. He wants them to know this could shake the very faith that has grown in each of them over the three years they have been together as Teacher and student. Jesus shares with them that there will be a part of Him that no one has seen, which goes by many names.

Helper.

Comforter.

Counselor.

Actually, what is coming is all of the above, and more. The Holy Spirit will arrive to minister not only to the disciples, but to anyone that has the faith to believe in Jesus as God's son.

For a while, the disciples will feel alone. Maybe even abandoned. But that won't last long. Their sorrow will soon turn to joy. That was part of the promise Jesus made to each of them.

His disciples.

His friends.

The ones Jesus loved.

John 16:1 The way we use words today may not have been exactly as they were used in biblical times. The word stumble here does not mean to trip and fall. The word stumble here should be likened to a person who walked on to a normal wood floor only for it to spring upward suddenly and catapult that person straight up and out of the room. The disciples weren't going to be asked to leave the synagogues. They were going to be taken by surprise and removed from this place of worship they had known their entire lives.

John 16:2 Amazingly enough, this would happen only a short while after Jesus's death and resurrection. Who was this person that would want to kill believers and claim it would be for God? Saul, who would later be known as Paul, would go on to write more letters in the New Testament than any other writer. Paul was also the greatest missionary we have ever known.

"I have said these things to you so that you wouldn't be caused to stumble. ² They will put you out of the synagogues. Yes, the time comes that whoever kills you will think that he offers service to God. ³ They will do these things because they have not known the Father, nor me. ⁴ But I have told you these things, so that when the time comes, you may remember that I told you about them. I didn't tell you these things from the beginning, because I was with you. ⁵ But now I am going to him who sent me, and none of you asks me, 'Where are you going?' ⁶ But because I have told you these things, sorrow has filled your heart. ⁷ Nevertheless I tell you the truth: It is to your advantage that I go away, for if I don't go away, the Counselor won't come to you. But if I go, I will send him to you. ⁸ When he has come, he will convict the world about sin, about righteousness, and about judgment; **9** about sin, because they don't believe in me; **10** about righteousness, because I am going to my Father, and you won't see me any more; **11** about judgment, because the prince of this world has been judged.

12 "I still have many things to tell you, but you can't bear them now. **13** However when he, the Spirit of truth, has come, he will guide you into all truth, for he will not speak from himself; but whatever he hears, he will speak. He will declare to you things that are coming. **14** He will glorify me, for he will take from what is mine, and will declare it to you. **15** All things that the Father has are mine; therefore I said that he takes of mine and will declare it to you. **16** A little while, and you will not see me. Again a little while, and you will see me."

17 Some of his disciples therefore said to one another, "What is this that he says to us, 'A little while, and you won't see me, and again a little while, and you will see me;' and, 'Because I go to the Father'?"

John 16:9-11 Jesus talks about three things that we no longer want to discuss: 1. Sin, which is missing the mark with God. 2. Righteousness, especially self-righteousness where we are all about our self and lost when it comes to doing the right thing before God. 3. Judgment, which is about condemning others and not about looking at situations through God's eyes. Through each of these, it is deciding what is right and what is wrong and choosing the right path because God shows us the right way.

John 16:12 Jesus is sharing with his closest friends that he will soon be walking to His death. The disciples are about to lose their teacher, their mentor, and their friend, and only Jesus knows what is about to happen. This is a human side to Jesus we often overlook: empathy. He is thinking about the disciples here and their feelings. Never be afraid to put yourself in the shoes of someone else to think for a moment how things look from where they stand, with all that is going on in their life.

John 16:20 The word sorrowful here is very specific to the disciples, who have seen the love of Jesus toward them and others, and the hatred directed toward their friend, Jesus. They will soon see their friend die along with everything and everyone that surrounds it. They will be sorrowful because the one they thought that could take the Romans out of power, and, in turn, bring them freedom, will be gone. As if losing their friend won't be enough, their sorrow will only grow when this happens, as all hope for them will seem to be gone.

John 16:20-22 In a way only Jesus can seem to accomplish, the sorrow they feel will be turned into the exact opposite: joy. With joy comes peace. With joy comes promise. With joy, their hope will return.

'A little while, and you won't see me, and again a little while, and you will see me;' and, 'Because I go to the Father'?" **18** They said therefore, "What is this that he says, 'A little while'? We don't know what he is saying."

19 Therefore Jesus perceived that they wanted to ask him, and he said to them, "Do you inquire among yourselves concerning this, that I said, 'A little while, and you won't see me, and again a little while, and you will see me?' **20** Most certainly I tell you that you will weep and lament, but the world will rejoice. You will be sorrowful, but your sorrow will be turned into joy. **21** A woman, when she gives birth, has sorrow because her time has come. But when she has delivered the child, she doesn't remember the anguish any more, for the joy that a human being is born into the world. **22** Therefore you now have sorrow, but I will see you again, and your heart will rejoice, and no one will take your joy away from you.

😮 23 "In that day you will ask me no questions. Most certainly I tell you, whatever you may ask of the Father in my name, he will give it to you. 24 Until now, you have asked nothing in my name. Ask, and you will receive, that your joy may be made full. 25 I have spoken these things to you in figures of speech. But the time is coming when I will no more speak to you in figures of speech, but will tell you plainly about the Father. 26 In that day you will ask in my name; and I himself loves you, don't say to you that I will pray to the Father for you, 27 for the Father because you have loved me, and have believed that I came from God. 28 I came from the Father, and have come into the world. Again, I leave the world, and go to the Father." 👍

29 His disciples said to him, "Behold, now you are speaking plainly, and using no figures of speech. 30 👍 Now we know that you know all things, and don't need for anyone to question you.

😮 John 16:23-27 Here we see the transition that takes place for the believer. Up to this point, a person had to go to a priest to speak to God. Jesus explained that was no longer the case: they could speak directly to God Himself. Jesus's death and resurrection gave us, as believers, direct access to our loving, Heavenly Father!

👍 John 16:28 If you have ever wanted to sum up the life and death of Jesus, this verse does it for you. It comes directly from Jesus himself: from God, to this world, to death, and back to His Heavenly Father.

👍 John 16:29-30 The disciples finally understood! It seemed as if Jesus was telling them the same thing over and over, and somehow, it finally sunk in and they understood.

John 16:31-33 Jesus didn't doubt the disciples' faith. Instead, he let them know what was about to come for each of them. They would run from this man they just said they believed in as God's one and only son. Jesus also assured them that would be ok. Despite their leaving, Jesus would not be alone as His Father would be with Him. And, in the end, the disciples would all find peace.

By this we believe that you came from God."

31 Jesus answered them, "Do you now believe? **32** Behold, the time is coming, yes, and has now come, that you will be scattered, everyone to his own place, and you will leave me alone. Yet I am not alone, because the Father is with me. **33** I have told you these things, that in me you may have peace. In the world you have trouble; but cheer up! I have overcome the world."

Introduction to Chapter 17

This entire chapter is a prayer of Jesus. Many today use the "Lord's Prayer" or "Our Father" (names we have given this prayer, not that Jesus gave to it) as the model of how to pray. You can find that prayer in Matthew 6:9-13 and Luke 11:2-4. The 17th chapter of John gives us a further example of how Jesus prayed to his Heavenly Father. It is filled with love and emotion from a son to his dad.

Throughout this gospel, Jesus shares that His "hour has not yet come". In this chapter, Jesus shares that His hour has finally arrived. How does Jesus handle that He will soon be walking to his death?

How each of us wishes we would.

Through prayer.

In this prayer, Jesus includes his disciples. Why? He knows He is leaving soon, and they will be left on their own. Jesus loves them so much He knows they need God's love in them to face what is about to come next. It will take God's love and strength to get the disciples through the next phase of their life: their own public ministry without Jesus walking alongside of them.

John 17 This entire chapter is a prayer from Jesus to his Heavenly Father. It is interesting that many times when we pray, we bow our heads and close our eyes. Here, Jesus gives the examples of having his eyes open as he looks up to heaven.

John 17:5 The very beginning of the Bible tells us the story of creation in Genesis. According to the account, man was made in "our image". In this prayer, Jesus shared that He was alongside of God before this world existed. So, who is part of the image in which you and I were made? Jesus.

Jesus said these things, then lifting up his eyes to heaven, he said, "Father, the time has come. Glorify your Son, that your Son may also glorify you; **2** even as you gave him authority over all flesh, so he will give eternal life to all whom you have given him. **3** This is eternal life, that they should know you, the only true God, and him whom you sent, Jesus Christ. **4** I glorified you on the earth. I have accomplished the work which you have given me to do. **5** Now, Father, glorify me with your own self with the glory which I had with you before the world existed. **6** I revealed your name to the people whom you have given me out of the world. They were yours, and you have given them to me. They have kept your word. **7** Now they have known that all things whatever you have given me are from you, **8** for the words which you have given me I have given to them, and they received them, and knew for sure that I came from you. They have believed that you sent me. **9** I pray for them. I don't pray for the world, but for those whom you have given me, for they are yours. **10** All things that are mine are yours, and yours are mine, and I am glorified in them. **11** I am no more in the world, but these are in the world, and I am coming to you. Holy Father, keep them through your name which you have given me, that they may be one, even as we are. **12** While I was with them in the world, I kept them in your name. I have kept those whom you have given me. None of them is lost except the son of destruction, that the Scripture might be fulfilled. **13** But now I come to you, and I say these things in the world, that they may have my joy made full in themselves. **14** I have given them your word. The world hated them, because they are not of the world, even as I am not of the world. **15** I pray not that you would take them from the world, but that you would

John 17:12 The "son of destruction" is also known as the "son of perdition" in some Bibles, which means he was punished for eternity for what he chose in this life. The son of destruction is Judas Iscariot. We will talk more about him in John 18. In the end, Judas chose to turn his back on Jesus. In the end, Judas never asked for forgiveness, once again by his choosing. The choices we make in this life determine where we choose to spend eternity. They can lead to destruction and perdition. They can also lead to paradise and heaven. But, make no mistake about it, the choice is yours and mine to make, and we can only choose for ourselves. Choose wisely.

John 17:13 Joy is a theme that is often repeated in the Gospel of John (See notes on John 15:11 and John 16:20-22). Jesus shares here that we can have the same joy that Jesus had, personally. This comes with our relationship with a personal Savior and a heavenly Father!

John 17:17 The word "sanctify" means to set apart, but it also means to be set apart for sacred use. As a believer, we are set apart by God and for God when we use the talents and gifts he has given us to reach and teach others. Jesus gave the disciples the word and wanted them to be sanctified – set apart for God's use – in the truth, which is God's Word.

John 17:21 Jesus prayed that the disciples wouldn't be seen as 11-12 separate believers, rather as one. The church, the body of Christ, the small groups, the ministries, the Bible Studies etc. all need to be united in the truth. Being one means we unite together, wherever there is two or more. Did you know that the only word in the English language that has the opposite meaning if you swap two letters is "unite"? Swap the "i" and the "t" and the word becomes "untie". Our focus as believers should always be to unite, as long as it is based on God's Truth.

keep them from the evil one. **16** They are not of the world even as I am not of the world. **17** Sanctify them in your truth. Your word is truth. **18** As you sent me into the world, even so I have sent them into the world. **19** For their sakes I sanctify myself, that they themselves also may be sanctified in truth. **20** Not for these only do I pray, but for those also who will believe in me through their word, **21** that they may all be one; even as you, Father, are in me, and I in you, that they also may be one in us; that the world may believe that you sent me. **22** The glory which you have given me, I have given to them; that they may be one, even as we are one; **23** I in them, and you in me, that they may be perfected into one; that the world may know that you sent me and loved them, even as you loved me. **24** Father, I desire that they also whom you have given me be with me where I am, that they may see my glory, which you given me, for you loved me before the foundation of the world **25** Righteous Father, the world hasn't known you, but I knew you; and these knew that you sent me. **26** I made known to them your name, and will make it known; that the love with which you loved me may be in them,

and I in them."

John 17:25-26 These two verses summarize the prayer that Jesus had in this chapter. It also summarized the relationship between Jesus and His Heavenly Father, and the offer that the same relationship is made available to each of us through God's love.

Introduction to Chapter 18

This is one of the saddest chapters in the Gospel of John. It is actually one of the saddest chapters in the entire Bible.

It starts with Jesus being betrayed by one of his best friends, Judas. He is arrested in a garden that Jesus and the disciples met at regularly.

The trial of the prisoner Jesus starts immediately. No trial is to be held at night according to the laws and customs of the Jews. That doesn't matter in the case of Jesus. They hate Him that much.

After drawing a sword and cutting off the ear of a servant, Peter goes on to deny Jesus three times in this chapter. At the end of Peter's third denial, a rooster crows, reminding Peter that Jesus had warned him this would take place.

Jesus is taken back and forth between the high priests. One is in charge. His name is Caiaphas. The other used to be in charge. His name is Annas. They are related and share in their hatred of this carpenter's son. Jesus finally comes before the man who has the most power in Jerusalem. His name is Pilate. He is Roman and hates his job, the city of Jerusalem, and most of all, its people. He can find no wrong in Jesus. Pilate knows Jesus is innocent. In the end, as is the Jews' custom at Passover every year, they get to pick between two criminals and one is released. The choices are Jesus and Barabbas, a robber that the people surely wouldn't want let go.

The people choose Barabbas to be set free.

CHAPTER 18

John 18:3 The detachment of soldiers here would have been Roman soldiers. The officers would have been the men that guarded (or policed) the temple every day.

John18:5 John didn't record the kiss that Judas gave to Jesus to greet him. He did record that Judas was "...standing with them." This is the first time that Judas publicly admitted that he was no longer on the same side with Jesus and the disciples. His betrayal of Jesus was now made known to everyone.

John 18:6 Jesus had already stated his seven "I am..." statements throughout the Gospel of John (See notes on John 6:35; John 8:12-9:5, John 10:7-10; John 10:11-14; John 14:6, John 15:1). Notice how everyone, including the soldiers and officers, reacted when Jesus said, "I am he." They stepped back and fell to the ground. Why? Even the non-believers recognized the great "I AM" and realized they were in the presence of God himself.

When Jesus had spoken these words, he went out with his disciples over the brook Kidron, where there was a garden, into which he and his disciples entered. ² Now Judas, who betrayed him, also knew the place, for Jesus often met there with his disciples. ³ Judas then, having taken a detachment of soldiers and officers from the chief priests and the Pharisees, came there with lanterns, torches, and weapons. ⁴ Jesus therefore, knowing all the things that were happening to him, went out, and said to them, "Who are you looking for?"

⁵ They answered him, "Jesus of Nazareth."

Jesus said to them, "I am he."

Judas also, who betrayed him, was standing with them.

⁶ When therefore he said to them, "I am he," they went backward, and fell to the ground.

⁷ Again therefore he asked them, "Who are you looking for?"

They said, "Jesus of Nazareth."

⁸ Jesus answered, "I told you that I am he. If therefore you seek me, let these go their way," ⁹ that the word might be fulfilled which he spoke, "Of those whom you have given me, I have lost none."

¹⁰ Simon Peter therefore, having a sword, drew it, struck the high priest's servant, and cut off his right ear. The servant's name was Malchus. ¹¹ Jesus therefore said to Peter, "Put the sword into its sheath. The cup which the Father has given me, shall I not surely drink it?"

¹² So the detachment, the commanding officer, and the officers of the Jews seized Jesus and bound him, ¹³ and led him to Annas first, for he was father-in-law to Caiaphas, who was high priest that year. ¹⁴ Now it was Caiaphas who advised the Jews that it was expedient that one man should perish for the people. ¹⁵ Simon Peter followed Jesus, as did another disciple. Now that disciple was

John 18:10 The only gospel that records the servant's name was John. Of all the people that would have been in the garden for the arrest of Jesus, the one that would not be armed would be the high priest's servant. And, of all the people Peter could have attacked, he chose the weakest one there, the one that wouldn't have been able to defend himself, as he was unarmed.

John 18:13 The high priest was the person in charge of leading the people to God. Annas was the high priest, which was a title for life, yet the Romans took him out of this office. The Romans replaced Annas with his son-in-law, Caiaphas. Both held the same title. The Jews saw Annas as the high priest. The Romans saw Caiaphas as the high priest.

John 18:14 Regardless of who was in charge, the Passover feast was the next day. Both high priests needed to get rid of Jesus, so they started His trial, illegally, after dark. They weren't just going to issue a warning, either. As Caiaphas shares in this verse, Jesus was going to receive the death penalty.

John 18:17 This is the first of Peter's three times that he will deny Christ. Jesus told Peter this would happen (See note on John 13:37-38).

John 18:17-18 We have all had bad days. But this has to rank up there as one of the worst days of all time. Peter had been told by Jesus that before this day (this really, really, really bad day) would end that Peter would deny Jesus three times. Here we see that not only did Peter deny him three times, but he did so this time where Jesus could hear him. And, what would Jesus see if he were to look at Peter? Peter warming himself, taking care of himself, and standing with the very people that were there to put Jesus to death.

known to the high priest, and entered in with Jesus into the court of the high priest; **16** but Peter was standing at the door outside. So the other disciple, who was known to the high priest, went out and spoke to her who kept the door, and brought in Peter. **17** Then the maid who kept the door said to Peter, "Are you also one of this man's disciples?"

He said, "I am not."

18 Now the servants and the officers were standing there, having made a fire of coals, for it was cold. They were warming themselves. Peter was with them, standing and warming himself. **19** The high priest therefore asked Jesus about his disciples and about his teaching. **20** Jesus answered him, "I spoke openly to the world. I always taught in synagogues, and in the temple, where the Jews always meet. I said nothing in secret. **21** Why do you ask me? Ask those who have heard me what I said to them. Behold, they know the things which I said."

22 When he had said this, one of the officers standing by slapped Jesus with his hand, saying, "Do you answer the high priest like that?"

23 Jesus answered him, "If I have spoken evil, testify of the evil; but if well, why do you beat me?"

24 Annas sent him bound to Caiaphas, the high priest. **25** Now Simon Peter was standing and warming himself. They said therefore to him, "You aren't also one of his disciples, are you?" He denied it and said, "I am not."

26 One of the servants of the high priest, being a relative of him whose ear Peter had cut off, said, "Didn't I see you in the garden with him?"

27 Peter therefore denied it again, and immediately the rooster crowed.

28 They led Jesus therefore from Caiaphas into the Praetorium. It was early, and they themselves didn't enter into the Praetorium, that they might

👍 John 18:23 The Old Testament taught "an eye for an eye". Jesus, however, taught to turn the other cheek. Just as Jesus stopped Peter in fighting in the garden for His sake (Read John 18:10-11), He would once again live this before the ones who were judging Him and putting Him on trial. Jesus's message was of peace and love, even when the world's message was about fighting and hatred.

John 18:25 This is the second of Peter's three times that he will deny Christ. (See notes on John 13:37-38 and John 18:17).

John 18:27 This was the third of Peter's three times that he denied Christ. This one came with a reminder, as Jesus had foretold Peter in John 13:38. After the third denial, the rooster crowed for all, specifically Peter, to hear.

John 18:28 The Praetorium was Pilate's home or palace. It was a military headquarter. Remember, Pilate was a Gentile. So, if the Jews followed Jesus into this area, they would be unclean, and couldn't eat the Passover meal. On the inside, in their hearts, the priests and other Jews were willing to have Jesus killed, which was against God's law. On the outside, they made sure to do all the right things in front of the other Jews, but couldn't take the chance they would miss out on the festival in case having Jesus killed didn't work into their schedules for that day.

John 18:33 The term "King" here was not a political term, but a religious one. If they called him a political king, he would be a threat to Pilate, and Pilate didn't see him as a threat. Instead, he was referring to Jesus as a religious king, which meant he was a threat to the Jews and their religious rules and ways. The King of the Jews literally means Messiah.

not be defiled, but might eat the Passover. **29** Pilate therefore went out to them, and said, "What accusation do you bring against this man?"

30 They answered him, "If this man weren't an evildoer, we wouldn't have delivered him up to you."

31 Pilate therefore said to them, "Take him yourselves, and judge him according to your law."

Therefore the Jews said to him, "It is illegal for us to put anyone to death," **32** that the word of Jesus might be fulfilled, which he spoke, signifying by what kind of death he should die.

33 Pilate therefore entered again into the Praetorium, called Jesus, and said to him, "Are you the King of the Jews?"

34 Jesus answered him, "Do you say this by yourself, or did others tell you about me?"

35 Pilate answered, "I'm not a Jew, am I? Your own nation and the chief priests delivered you to me. What have you done?"

36 Jesus answered, "My Kingdom is not of this world. If my Kingdom were of this world, then my servants would fight, that I wouldn't be delivered to the Jews. But now my Kingdom is not from here."

37 Pilate therefore said to him, "Are you a king then?"

Jesus answered, "You say that I am a king. For this reason I have been born, and for this reason I have come into the world, that I should testify to the truth. Everyone who is of the truth listens to my voice."

38 Pilate said to him, "What is truth?"

When he had said this, he went out again to the Jews, and said to them, "I find no basis for a charge against him. **39** But you have a custom, that I should release someone to you at the Passover. Therefore, do you want me to release to you the King of the Jews?"

40 Then they all shouted again, saying, "Not this man, but Barabbas!" Now Barabbas was a robber.

John 18:38 Truth is a moving target for many in the political world. For Pilate, truth meant whatever would keep the most people happy, which would help him keep his job. He hated the people of Jerusalem, but he also loved the power of ruling over them. To keep that power, doing what was popular may win out over what or who stood for the truth.

John 18:40 This was a perfect example of the popular choice winning out over the truth. Pilate was sure the Jews would choose the innocent man, Jesus, over the criminal, Barabbas. Pilate was wrong, and it would haunt him for the rest of his life.

Introduction to Chapter 19

This is the chapter Jesus dies. After being mocked verbally by the soldiers, a crown of thorns is placed on his head. It is another way to make fun of Jesus, this time as a "king".

Pilate is struggling with the decision to have Jesus killed. He knows Jesus has done nothing wrong. In the end, he chooses to listen to the crowd. They are an angry mob, thirsty for blood. Not just any blood either; they want Jesus's blood.

Pilate does have one final say in the matter. However, it doesn't deal with saving Jesus's life. Instead, he has a sign made that every passer by can read. "JESUS OF NAZARETH, KING OF THE JEWS" is placed above the head of Jesus on the cross.

The Jews argue with what is written. Pilate stands firm with what is already on the sign. It is placed on the cross above His head, and Pilate's soldiers make sure of it.

Jesus announces His own death with "It is finished!" His body is pierced in the side to make sure He is gone. His legs are left unbroken, and His body is taken and placed in the tomb of a Jew, by a rich Jewish man and the man that had once come to Jesus at night, Nicodemus. He helps the rich man, Joseph of Arimathea, prepare Jesus's body for burial.

The day ends in silence with His death.

John 19:4 Pilate had Jesus beaten yet he had the power to release him, thinking the beating would be enough for the crowd of people there wanting to see Jesus suffer. His poor choices would continue, as he would repeatedly listen to the voices of an angry mob. It is so easy to give into the crowd. In the end, always remember, there is never a wrong time to choose to make the right decision.

John 19:6-41 The word crucify (or past tense crucified) appears for the first time in chapter 19, where it is found more than ten times. This shows us the Jews already had a plan in place to deliver a death, by law, only the Romans could deliver.

CHAPTER 19

So Pilate then took Jesus, and flogged him. ² The soldiers twisted thorns into a crown, and put it on his head, and dressed him in a purple garment. ³ They kept saying, "Hail, King of the Jews!" and they kept slapping him.

⁴ Then Pilate went out again, and said to them, "Behold, I bring him out to you, that you may know that I find no basis for a charge against him."

⁵ Jesus therefore came out, wearing the crown of thorns and the purple garment. Pilate said to them, "Behold, the man!"

⁶ When therefore the chief priests and the officers saw him, they shouted, saying, "Crucify! Crucify!"

Pilate said to them, "Take him yourselves, and crucify him, for I find no basis for a charge against him."

⁷ The Jews answered him, "We have a law, and by our law he ought to die, because he made himself the Son of God." ⁸ When

therefore Pilate heard this saying, he was more afraid. [9] He entered into the Praetorium again, and said to Jesus, "Where are you from?" But Jesus gave him no answer. [10] Pilate therefore said to him, "Aren't you speaking to me? Don't you know that I have power to release you and have power to crucify 😐 you?"

[11] Jesus answered, "You would have no power at all against me, unless it were given to you from above. Therefore he who delivered me to you has greater sin."

[12] At this, Pilate was seeking to release him, but the Jews cried out, saying, "If you release this man, you aren't Caesar's friend! Everyone who makes himself a king speaks against Caesar!" 😮

[13] When Pilate therefore heard these words, he brought Jesus out and sat down on the judgment seat at a place called "The Pavement", but in Hebrew, "Gabbatha." [14] Now it was the Preparation Day of the Passover,

😐 John 19:10 There was no word to share the kind of pain that Jesus was about to go through when the Romans had Jesus crucified. To describe this type of intense, nearly unbearable pain, the word "excruciating" was added to the English language. The pain in this word comes from the word crucify, or crucifixion.

😮 John 19:12 History tells us that Pilate was on bad terms with the Roman Emperor. He used excessive force with the Jews and the complaints got back to Rome. Ruling over this city and its people was a slap in the face, to Pilate. Still, he had to keep the people happy if he were to ever get back in the good graces of those who ruled over him. When the people cried out that he would no longer be a friend of Caesar, Pilate caved to the pressure. When Pilate chose to please the people, he chose to kill the very Son of God in the same process. His position and power were more important to him than doing the right thing. Remember: there is never a wrong time to do the right thing for God.

John 19:15 For over 400 years, God had been silent to the Jews. Generation after generation had been looking for the Messiah, and had died waiting for God to deliver them from the Romans. God finally sent His son to deliver them, but, in the end, they chose the people in power over God's one and only Son. In this verse, they even cried out publicly that their king was not God, but a Roman emperor.

John 19:20 The reason that Jesus's title was written in three languages is that the place of the crucifixion was outside the city walls of Jerusalem in a public area, quite possibly a busy trade route. This would demonstrate to any and everyone that passed through the power of the Roman military. By writing the title in these three languages, the most used in this area of the world, any passer by would be able to read it.

at about the sixth hour. He said to the Jews, "Behold, your King!" 15 They cried out, "Away with him! Away with him! Crucify him!"

Pilate said to them, "Shall I crucify your King?"

The chief priests answered, "We have no king but Caesar!"

16 So then he delivered him to them to be crucified. So they took Jesus and led him away. 17 He went out, bearing his cross, to the place called "The Place of a Skull", which is called in Hebrew, "Golgotha", 18 where they crucified him, and with him two others, on either side one, and Jesus in the middle. 19 Pilate wrote a title also, and put it on the cross. There was written, "JESUS OF NAZARETH, THE KING OF THE JEWS." 20 Therefore many of the Jews read this title, for the place where Jesus was crucified was near the city; and it was written in Hebrew, in Latin, and in Greek. 21 The chief priests of the Jews therefore said to Pilate, "Don't write, 'The King

of the Jews,' but, 'he said, "I am King of the Jews." ' "22 Pilate answered, "What I have written, I have written."

23 Then the soldiers, when they had crucified Jesus, took his garments and made four parts, to every soldier a part; and also the coat. Now the coat was without seam, woven from the top throughout. 👍 24 Then they said to one another, "Let's not tear it, but cast lots for it to decide whose it will be," that the Scripture might be fulfilled, which says, "They parted my garments among them. For my cloak they cast lots." Therefore the soldiers did these things. 🙁

25 But standing by Jesus' cross were his mother, his mother's sister, Mary the wife of Clopas, and Mary Magdalene. 26 Therefore when Jesus saw his mother, and the disciple whom he loved #️⃣ standing there, he said to his mother, "Woman 👍, behold, your son!" 27 Then he said to the disciple, "Behold, your mother!" From that hour, the

142

👍 John 19:23 The coat without seam was a very significant statement. To the Jews, the one who wore the coat (or tunic) without seam was the High Priest (Exodus 28:31-32).

🙁 John 19:24 God's one and only Son is dying on the cross, and the Roman soldiers are below him gambling for His clothes. The soldiers didn't even realize they were fulfilling Scripture (Psalm 22:18), which further indicates that Jesus was, in fact, the Messiah the Jews had been looking for all this time.

#️⃣ John 19:26 "The disciple Jesus loved" is the author of this book, John. He isn't saying that Jesus loved him only, nor is he sharing this in a sense of pride or arrogance. John shares this in humility that he is one of many that Jesus loves personally. He uses the title "the disciple Jesus loved" five times in this Gospel (John 13:23; 19:26, 20:2, 21:7, and 21:20). It is found nowhere else in the Bible.

👍 John 19:26 When Jesus uses the term "Woman..." it is not a sign of disrespect as it would be in our society today. In this culture, it is a sign of complete respect. It would be like us saying "Madam", "Miss", or "Mrs.".

John 19:30 The vinegar, or sour wine, was not a wine to numb the senses for the men dying on the cross. It took hours for prisoners to die on the cross. The Romans had to send a message to the Jews, the public, and anyone passing by, and it was a serious one that played out over the day. The drink Jesus took was actually what the soldiers used to drink during this long day of work. It allowed Him to moisten his throat to make one clear, final statement in His earthly ministry: not an announcement of defeat, but one of completion.

John 19:34 Some people want to understand the science of the Bible. This is a great example of science showing up without us taking the time to recognize it. Over time, theories have surfaced that Jesus was in a coma, in a trance, or was just unconscious on the cross. In all three of these cases, the blood would still be flowing through His body. When the soldier pierced the side of Jesus, it clearly states that both "blood and water came out". The only way the blood and water could come out was if it were separated, indicating it was no longer flowing through His body, meaning He was scientifically dead.

disciple took her to his own home. **28** After this, Jesus, seeing that all things were now finished, that the Scripture might be fulfilled, said, "I am thirsty." **29** Now a vessel full of vinegar was set there; so they put a sponge full of the vinegar on hyssop, and held it at his mouth. **30** When Jesus therefore had received the vinegar , he said, "It is finished." Then he bowed his head, and gave up his spirit. **31** Therefore the Jews, because it was the Preparation Day, so that the bodies wouldn't remain on the cross on the Sabbath (for that Sabbath was a special one), asked of Pilate that their legs might be broken, and that they might be taken away. **32** Therefore the soldiers came, and broke the legs of the first, and of the other who was crucified with him; **33** but when they came to Jesus, and saw that he was already dead, they didn't break his legs. **34** However one of the soldiers pierced his side with a spear, and immediately blood and water came out.

35 He who has seen has testified, and his testimony is true. He knows that he tells the truth, that you may believe. 36 For these things happened that the Scripture might be fulfilled, "A bone of him will not be broken." 37 Again another Scripture says, "They will look on him whom they pierced." 38 After these things, Joseph of Arimathaea, being a disciple of Jesus, but secretly for fear of the Jews, asked of Pilate that he might take away Jesus' body. Pilate gave him permission. He came therefore and took away his body. 39 Nicodemus, who at first came to Jesus by night, also came bringing a mixture of myrrh and aloes, about a hundred Roman pounds. 40 So they took Jesus' body, and bound it in linen cloths with the spices, as the custom of the Jews is to bury. 41 Now in the place where he was crucified there was a garden. In the garden was a new tomb in which no man had ever yet been laid. 42 Then because of the Jews' Preparation Day (for the tomb was near at hand) they laid Jesus there.

John 19:36-37 Notice what John shares in these verses: he states that "Scripture" would be fulfilled. He doesn't share that these fulfilled a prophecy (or basically a prediction). Verse 36 fulfills what John the Baptizer (or Baptist) stated in John 1;29, and also from the Old Testament in Exodus 12:42 and Psalm 34:20. John 19:37 points to Zechariah 12:10.

John 19:38-39 Which disciples came to take Jesus's body to have him buried? None of the original 12 disciples did so. Instead, two well known, wealthy, highly respected Jews in Joseph of Arimathaea and Nicodemus. That is how much they loved their friend, Jesus, that they would risk everything for their friend and savior.

Introduction to Chapter 20

There is a time lapse between the 19th and 20th chapters of the Gospel of John. Chapter 19 ended on Friday, which was the day Jesus died. Chapter 20 started on Sunday, which was the day that they found the empty tomb.

The disciples all went to the tomb to see that it was empty. When they found it empty, what did they do next?

They went home. Not Mary Magdalene, who found the stone in front of the tomb, had been rolled away. She stayed and wept. What did she see next? Two angels. And then she saw the risen Jesus. She went and shared this with the disciples.

Later that same day Jesus appeared in the middle of the disciples. The disciples were hiding in a large room with the doors shut when Jesus appeared. What did Jesus say to them?

"Peace."

Jesus promised peace to the disciples when He talked to them about this day in John chapter 14. The offer never changed.

The chapter ends with Thomas getting the nickname he has carried through history. He was the "doubter". It also ends with the reason John wrote the very book that bears not only his name, but, the love of Jesus.

John 20:1 The first day of the week was Sunday. Jesus died on a Friday. That means it was only two days, right? Not in the Jewish culture. Luke (23:44-49) records that Jesus died somewhere between the 6th and 9th hour of the day. That would be between noon (the 6th hour as their day started at 6 a.m.) and 3 p.m. If something happened at any part of the day, it was considered an actual day. So, when Jesus died between 12-3 p.m., that was Friday. When all was quiet the entire next day; that was Saturday. When Mary and the others showed up to start the next day, just before the sun was coming up, which would have been the first hour (between 6 a.m. to 7 a.m.) on Sunday. The total number of hours would be between 40-43 hours, or less than two full days. Once again, in this culture, once an event took place at any part of the day, in this case the first hour, that was the third day.

Now on the first day of the week , Mary Magdalene went early, while it was still dark, to the tomb, and saw the stone taken away from the tomb. **2** Therefore she ran and came to Simon Peter and to the other disciple whom Jesus loved, and said to them, "They have taken away the Lord out of the tomb, and we don't know where they have laid him!"

3 Therefore Peter and the other disciple went out, and they went toward the tomb. **4** They both ran together. The other disciple outran Peter, and came to the tomb first. **5** Stooping and looking in, he saw the linen cloths lying, yet he didn't enter in. **6** Then Simon Peter came, following him, and entered into the tomb. He saw the linen cloths lying, **7** and the cloth that had been on his head, not lying with the linen cloths, but rolled up in a place by itself. **8** So then the other disciple who came first to the tomb also entered in, and he saw and believed. **9** For as yet they didn't know the Scripture, that he must rise from the dead. **10** So the disciples went away again to their own homes. **11** But Mary was standing outside at the tomb weeping. So as she wept, she stooped and looked into the tomb, **12** and she saw two angels in white sitting, one at the head, and one at the feet, where the body of Jesus had lain. **13** They asked her, "Woman, why are you weeping?"

She said to them, "Because they have taken away my Lord, and I don't know where they have laid him." **14** When she had said this, she turned around and saw Jesus standing, and didn't know that it was Jesus.

15 Jesus said to her, "Woman, why are you weeping? Who are you looking for?"

She, supposing him to be the gardener, said to him, "Sir, if you have carried him away, tell me where you have laid him, and I will take him away."

16 Jesus said to her, "Mary."

John 20:12 Matthew and Mark reveal one angel, while Luke and John reveal two angels. Which was it? Either one is correct. Angels reveal themselves when they choose to. Notice that the disciples didn't see the angels when they looked into the tomb, but they suddenly appeared to Mary. We don't understand or know how. But, for all who believe, one day when we are in Heaven we may finally know the reason.

John 20:12 John records that two angels were present when Mary was at the tomb. When Satan left Heaven, he took 1/3 of the angels with him to do his dirty work. That means the final 2/3 of the angels are watching over us. In this case, the two angels that watched over Jesus (who was standing behind Mary at this time) could very well be His Guardian Angels (this term is not in the Bible) for His time here with us.

John 20:19-21 It was interesting that in a locked room Jesus suddenly showed up in the middle of the disciples. They were in the locked room because of their fear of the Jews. So what is the first thing Jesus offered to each of them as they cowered in fear? Peace. And Jesus offered it not once, but twice. God's peace will always win over this world's fear! Jesus promised each of us that! (See note on John 14:27).

John 20:21 Here we see the ministry of Jesus being passed to the disciples. Remember, the disciples had to be discipled for three years before they were ready to disciple others. Make no mistake about it, this is what Jesus intended for them and intends for each of us today with our lives. We learn from Him, live through Him, and love others because He first loved us. This is how and why Jesus's ministry has grown and lasted for thousands of years after His death and resurrection.

She turned and said to him, "Rabboni!" which is to say, "Teacher!"

17 Jesus said to her, "Don't hold me, for I haven't yet ascended to my Father; but go to my brothers and tell them, 'I am ascending to my Father and your Father, to my God and your God.' "

18 Mary Magdalene came and told the disciples that she had seen the Lord, and that he had said these things to her. **19** When therefore it was evening on that day, the first day of the week, and when the doors were locked where the disciples were assembled, for fear of the Jews, Jesus came and stood in the middle, and said to them, "Peace be to you."

20 When he had said this, he showed them his hands and his side. The disciples therefore were glad when they saw the Lord. **21** Jesus therefore said to them again, "Peace be to you. As the Father has sent me, even so I send you." **22** When he had said this, he breathed on them, and said to them, "Receive the Holy Spirit! **23** If you forgive anyone's sins, they have been forgiven them. If you retain anyone's sins, they have been retained."

24 But Thomas, one of the twelve, called Didymus, wasn't with them when Jesus came. **25** The other disciples therefore said to him, "We have seen the Lord!" But he said to them, "Unless I see in his hands the print of the nails, put my finger into the print of the nails, and put my hand into his side, I will not believe."

26 After eight days again his disciples were inside and Thomas was with them. Jesus came, the doors being locked, and stood in the middle, and said, "Peace be to you." **27** Then he said to Thomas, "Reach here your finger, and see my hands. Reach here your hand, and put it into my side. Don't be unbelieving, but believing."

28 Thomas answered him, "My Lord and my God!"

John 20:25-29
Thomas is often criticized for this statement. It is where the term "Doubting Thomas" was born. Let's look at it a little differently. Could it be that Thomas was courageous enough to speak what everyone else was thinking? Thomas never actually touched Jesus and his wounds, because by seeing, he believed. At the same time, when Thomas had the courage to speak up on a subject, God showed him something that only God could show. Be bold in your requests to God, and see how God responds to them. But don't confuse doubt with courage!

👍 John 20:27-29 The book of John was written to the Gentiles. During Biblical times, a Gentile was anyone that was not a Jew (see note on John 1:1). Who exactly was it written to? In the words of Jesus: to anyone who had not seen his miracles and signs and still believed.

\# John 20:31 One of the central themes of the Gospel of John is "believe". It shows up nearly 100 times in this gospel alone, more than the other three gospels combined, and nearly 1/3 of the total number of times in the entire Bible!

²⁹ Jesus said to him, "Because you have seen me, you have believed. Blessed are those who have not seen, and have believed." 👍

³⁰ Therefore Jesus did many other signs in the presence of his disciples, which are not written in this book; ³¹ but these are written, that you may believe. \# that Jesus is the Christ, the Son of God, and that believing you may have life in his name.

Introduction to Chapter 21

This is the final chapter of the Gospel of John, but far from the end of the story about Jesus. 😤 Jesus shows the disciples what he has shared with him from the beginning of their ministry, that He would never leave them, nor forsake them.

What is the first thing Jesus does when he finds them all together fishing, as most of them grew up doing? He has a meal with them. What we know as the Last Supper was had before his death. What we read about here is the breakfast they share which they have on this early morning after his resurrection. 😕

We also get to see Jesus restore Peter, even though he denied Jesus three times the day of his death. His instructions to Peter are the same instructions to all of the disciples: feed, tend, and love the lambs and the sheep. Jesus ends this conversation with the same command He gave the disciples when He first called them to their public ministry: "Follow Me." 😮

How did the disciples respond? By comparing themselves to each other. 😳😠 Jesus shares that our calling is our calling, and each of us, individually, chooses to follow that path and His lead.

As John closes, he reminds us that there is so much more to Jesus that we can't understand. His compassion, His empathy, His healing, and His acts of kindness are as endless as His love for each one of us. Not this book, nor any book, could contain all the love Jesus has for you and me. 👍😌

John 21:3 We can all relate to Peter. Jesus has revealed himself to the disciples. But Peter can't get past the fact he denied Jesus three times. So what does he do? He goes back to what he knows the best. In Peter's case it is his work. It can be any number of things that keep us away from our savior. Smart phones, video games, movies, binge watching, music, sports, addictions, these are all examples of areas that control us away from God. None of these are bad by themselves. But, if they cause us to focus on ourselves, they take us away from the one who wants to walk alongside of us every step of the way, every single day. Be aware!

John 21:7 Hopefully, this is a way we one day can relate to Peter, as well. When he heard that it was Jesus, Peter didn't wait. He left what he was doing immediately and threw himself in the direction of Jesus. It was early morning. The water would have been very cold. It didn't matter to Peter. What mattered was that Jesus was on the shore and Peter was in the boat and Peter just had to get to him.

CHAPTER 21

After these things, Jesus revealed himself again to the disciples at the sea of Tiberias. He revealed himself this way. ² Simon Peter, Thomas called Didymus, Nathanael of Cana in Galilee, and the sons of Zebedee, and two others of his disciples were together. ³ Simon Peter said to them, "I'm going fishing."

They told him, "We are also coming with you." They immediately went out, and entered into the boat. That night, they caught nothing. ⁴ But when day had already come, Jesus stood on the beach, yet the disciples didn't know that it was Jesus. ⁵ Jesus therefore said to them, "Children, have you anything to eat?"

They answered him, "No."

⁶ He said to them, "Cast the net on the right side of the boat, and you will find some."

They cast it therefore, and now they weren't able to draw it in for the multitude of fish. ⁷ That disciple therefore whom

Jesus loved said to Peter, "It's the Lord!"

So when Simon Peter heard that it was the Lord, he wrapped his coat around himself (for he was naked), and threw himself into the sea. **8** But the other disciples came in the little boat (for they were not far from the land, but about two hundred cubits away), dragging the net full of fish. **9** So when they got out on the land, they saw a fire of coals there, with fish and bread laid on it. **10** Jesus said to them, "Bring some of the fish which you have just caught."

11 Simon Peter went up, and drew the net to land, full of one hundred fifty-three great fish. Even though there were so many, the net wasn't torn.

12 Jesus said to them, "Come and eat breakfast!"

None of the disciples dared inquire of him, "Who are you?" knowing that it was the Lord.

13 Then Jesus came and took the bread, gave it to them, and the fish likewise. **14** This is now the third time that Jesus was

John 21:8 Ever wonder how far or long a cubit is? If you hold out your arm, it is roughly the distance from the end of your finger to your elbow. For most people that is about 18 inches (or about 46 centimeters) in length! If Jesus was 200 cubits from the disciples, that means Peter swam about 300 feet (100 yards), which is the same length as a football field without the end zones.

John 21:9-10 Where did the fish on the fire come from since the disciples hadn't even brought the net full of fish on to the shore at this point? This shows that God can do things at any time on His own without us. Jesus invites the disciples to bring some of the fish to join in the meal they are about to have together. God can do it alone, but He is a relational God. He wants us to join with Him and take part!

John 21:15-18 Jesus starts the conversation with Peter the same way he spoke to him when they first met: "Simon, son of Jonah". It's a reminder of who he is. After asking him three times about Peter's love for Him, Jesus instructs Peter with three words to show that love: feed, tend, and feed once again. Saying you love someone is one thing. Showing it by feeding, tending, calling, helping, meeting, etc. will make you do as Jesus called each of us that choose to follow Him: be fishers of men. (Matthew 4:19)

John 21:15-17 Who are we to love and tend to every day? We are to love the lamb and the sheep. Regardless of race, gender, religious background, political affiliation, etc., we are to reach out and care for both the young and the old.

revealed to his disciples after he had risen from the dead. **15** So when they had eaten their breakfast, Jesus said to Simon Peter, "Simon, son of Jonah, do you love me more than these?"

He said to him, "Yes, Lord; you know that I have affection for you."

He said to him, "Feed my lambs." **16** He said to him again a second time, "Simon, son of Jonah, do you love me?"

He said to him, "Yes, Lord; you know that I have affection for you."

He said to him, "Tend my sheep." **17** He said to him the third time, "Simon, son of Jonah, do you have affection for me?"

Peter was grieved because he asked him the third time, "Do you have affection for me?" He said to him, "Lord, you know everything. You know that I have affection for you."

Jesus said to him, "Feed my sheep. **18** Most certainly I tell you, when you were young, you dressed yourself and walked where you wanted to. But when you are old, you will stretch out your hands, and another will dress you and carry you where you don't want to go."

19 Now he said this, signifying by what kind of death he would Glorify God. When he had said this, he said to him, "Follow me."

👍 John 21:19 Jesus's first command was the same as his last command to his disciples: "Follow Me." Disciples have to make the decision to do so.

20 Then Peter, turning around, saw a disciple following. This was the disciple whom Jesus loved, the one who had also leaned on Jesus' breast at the supper and asked, "Lord, who is going to betray you?" **21** Peter seeing him, said to Jesus, "Lord, what about this man?"

22 Jesus said to him, "If I desire that he stay until I come, what is that to you? You follow me." 😮

23 This saying therefore went out among the brothers, that this disciple wouldn't die. Yet Jesus didn't say to him that he wouldn't die, but, "If I desire that he stay until I come, what is that to you?"

😮 John 21:20-22 Jesus and Peter just had this great conversation about loving and tending to others, and what is the first thing Peter does? He wants to know what Jesus is going to do with John, the writer of this book and one of the other disciples. This is so typical of each of us. We are always comparing ourselves to others in many different ways. Jesus doesn't tell Peter what will happen to John, but instead points out that it doesn't really matter to Peter. It is up to Peter to choose to follow Jesus, just as it is up to John, and you, and me, to follow Jesus. Be careful not to get stuck in the comparison game. Instead of asking God "What about...." in regards to someone else, get in the practice of asking God "What next?" and keep the focus on your personal walk with Him!

John 21:24-25 The Gospel of John was written to show, from a first hand witness, friend, and follower of Jesus, that Jesus was the Son of God. When you read this gospel, you see the good news that God is a relational, loving God. After reading it, each of us has to determine whether or not we believe. Make no mistake about it; the choice is a personal one, between you and God. When you go back and read this gospel, and consider who wrote it, and why, may you believe as so many others do that God sent his one and only son not to only love the world, but to love you so that you would have eternal life (See note on John 3:16).

24 This is the disciple who testifies about these things, and wrote these things. We know that his witness is true. **25** There are also many other things which Jesus did, which if they would all be written, I suppose that even the world itself wouldn't have room for the books that would be written.

Additional copies of EMOJIs and the Gospel of John can be ordered on the following website:

www.PocketFullOfFaith.com